Better Homes and Gardens®

step-by-step
low-maintenance gardens

Patricia Taylor

Better Homes and Gardens® Books
Des Moines, Iowa

Better Homes and Gardens® Books
An imprint of Meredith® Books

Step-by-Step Low-Maintenance Gardens
Senior Editor: Marsha Jahns
Production Manager: Douglas Johnston

Vice President and Editorial Director: Elizabeth P. Rice
Executive Editor: Kay Sanders
Art Director: Ernest Shelton
Managing Editor: Christopher Cavanaugh

President, Book Group: Joseph J. Ward
Vice President, Retail Marketing: Jamie L. Martin
Vice President, Direct Marketing: Timothy Jarrell

Meredith Corporation
Chairman of the Executive Committee: E. T. Meredith III
Chairman of the Board and Chief Executive Officer:
    Jack D. Rehm
President and Chief Operating Officer: William T. Kerr

Produced by ROUNDTABLE PRESS, INC.
Directors: Susan E. Meyer, Marsha Melnick
Executive Editor: Amy T. Jonak
Editorial Director: Anne Halpin
Senior Editor: Jane Mintzer Hoffman
Design: Brian Sisco, Susan Evans, Sisco & Evans, New York
Photo Editor: Marisa Bulzone
Assistant Photo Editor: Carol Sattler
Encyclopedia Editor: Henry W. Art and Storey
    Communications, Inc., Pownal, Vermont
Horticultural Consultant: Christine M. Douglas
Copy Editor: Sue Heinemann
Proofreader: Cathy Peck
Assistant Editor: Alexis Wilson
Step-by-Step Photography: Derek Fell
Garden Plans: Elayne Sears and Storey Communications, Inc.

All of us at Meredith® Books are dedicated to providing you
with the information and ideas you need for successful gardening. We guarantee your satisfaction with this book for as
long as you own it. If you have any questions, comments, or
suggestions, please write to us at:

Meredith® Books, *Garden Books*
Editorial Department, LN112
1716 Locust St.
Des Moines, IA 50309–3023

STEP-BY-STEP

Low-Maintenance Gardens

5 INTRODUCTION
What Is Low-Maintenance Gardening?

11 CHAPTER ONE
Designing for Lower Maintenance

Soil Types, 12 Light, 14 Moisture, 15 Hardiness and Climate, 16 Plant Groupings, 18 Lawns and
Ground Covers, 19 Shrub Borders, 23 Foliage, 26 Vegetables, 28 Paths, 30 Hot and Dry Conditions, 32
Wet Conditions, 37 Seashore Conditions, 41

Garden Plans

Lazy Gardener's Bed, 46 Easy-Care Formal Garden, 48 Weekend-Home Garden, 50 Kitchen Garden, 52

55 CHAPTER TWO
Low-Maintenance Plants

Trees and Shrubs, 56 Perennials, 60 Annuals, 63 Bulbs, 66 Ornamental Grasses, 68 Herbs, 70 Vegetables, 72

75 CHAPTER THREE
Techniques That Lower Maintenance

Soil, 76 Planting, 80 Watering, 84 Weeding, 87 Pruning, 89 Pest Control, 92 Regional Calendar of
Garden Care, 96

98 ENCYCLOPEDIA OF PLANTS
Low-Maintenance Plants

127 PLANT HARDINESS ZONE MAP

128 RESOURCES FOR LOW-MAINTENANCE GARDENS

130 INDEX

What Is Low-Maintenance Gardening?

*l*ow-maintenance gardening is commonsense gardening. You just put the right plants in the right place, and then relax while your garden essentially thrives on its own. Planning ahead is the key. • Before you put the spade into the ground, create a design scheme to ensure a harmonious arrangement of plants. Analyze your proposed garden site, and choose fuss-free plants whose cultural needs match your growing conditions. With this strategy you will enjoy a beautiful, productive low-maintenance garden. • Step by step, this book shows you how to create a lovely minimal-work garden and choose suitable plants. You will learn valuable timesaving maintenance techniques that will reduce your gardening chores and make gardening a pleasure. The result will be an easy-care garden that is a continual source of delight.

For much of history, planting and maintaining a garden have had little to do with the resulting display of plants. Ornamental gardens were traditionally a sign of wealth, requiring hordes of workers to care for the extravagant plantings.

In the early 1800s, for example, the Duke of Wellington created what was popularly known as an "American garden" at his estate in Stratfield Saye, southwest of London. It mattered little that many of the American rhododendrons and mountain laurels planted there required hot summers and cold winters and were thus totally unsuited to the British climate; a large staff toiled incessantly to pamper the plants so that they would flower. (Today, most of the plants at the duke's estate have been replaced with the heaths that are better suited to England's climate and soil.)

By the mid-1800s, the economic growth caused by the Industrial Revolution began to change the notion that gardening was only for the upper class. A middle class emerged that wanted to copy the gardening practices of the opulent elite but couldn't afford a staff of laborers. At the same time, the supply of garden help diminished as millions of workers took factory jobs that paid better than estate work.

For the next century gardens became low-maintenance by default, but they also became very dull. American gardens consisted of a foundation of an evergreen shrub—a yew, an arborvitae, or occasionally, a rhododendron or azalea—next to the house. Every spring, a few rows of annuals were placed in the middle of a lawn or along a border. Heavy doses of pesticides were applied weekly to keep insects from destroying the plants.

In 1962 the environmental movement was born, spurred in large part by the publication of Rachel Carson's *Silent Spring*. Stressing the interrelatedness

Ornamental grasses combine with low-maintenance perennials in a durable, easy-care garden.

Ornamental grasses bring form, texture, and movement to low-maintenance gardens all summer, but they really come into their own in autumn, when their feathery flowers and seedheads dance gaily in the breeze.

*The first rule of low-mainte-
nance gardening is to choose
plants that are suited to the
growing conditions where
you live. In a hot, dry climate where rainfall is scarce,
a garden of cacti and succulents is ideal.*

*Even a rock garden can be
undemanding of the gar-
dener's time and effort when
the plants are carefully
chosen. Compact succulents
join with drought-tolerant
agaves (Agave spp.) and cacti
in this rock garden in the
West, where summers are
hot and arid.*

of plant and animal life, this landmark book height-
ened many people's awareness of the harmful effects
of pesticides and encouraged using plants that did not
need to be sprayed with toxic insecticides and fungi-
cides in order to thrive. Breeders and nurseries
responded by offering more plants that were easy to
care for and resistant to pests and diseases.

These sturdy, easy-to-care-for plants became commercially available around the time that baby boomers
began to discover the joys of gardening. For a genera-
tion characterized by busy lifestyles and a wish to have
it all, low-maintenance gardens provided a handsome
setting for little work.

In the 1970s Washington, DC, architects Wolfgang
Oehme and James Van Sweden created the "New
American Garden," one that is beautiful throughout
the entire year and yet requires minimal maintenance.

Following Oehme and Van Sweden's tradition,
beauty is never sacrificed in the low-maintenance gardening techniques and plants described in this book.
An easy-care garden can have plenty of color, and also
interesting sculptural forms and textures. In fuss-free
gardens pesticides are rarely used and fertilization is
kept to a minimum. The gardener is rewarded with
abundant harvests and gorgeous plants.

This bounty does not come about by chance. A considerable amount of thought is given to the low-maintenance garden before planting takes place so that
only minimal work is required afterward. Using the
low-maintenance gardening techniques covered in this
book, anyone can enjoy the pleasure and bounty of
wonderful plants, even within the limitations imposed
by a busy lifestyle. This is the satisfying rather than
the frustrating way to garden.

CHAPTER 1

Designing for Lower Maintenance

*g*ood design is a crucial element in producing low-maintenance, easy-care gardens. Designing a garden doesn't mean you have to place plants perfectly in elegant formal settings. Nor does garden design necessarily require a lot of work, although you do need some knowledge. • By thoroughly understanding the kind of setting in which you are gardening, you will be able to choose plants that will thrive with little work on your part. You can just sit back and enjoy their beauty and bounty. • This chapter gives you the information you need to plan a low-maintenance garden.

Soil Types

Invasive Plants

These attractive plants soon become uncontrolled weeds when planted in good garden soil. Be wary of planting them unless you can find methods to confine them.

Trumpet creeper (Campsis radicans) Vine with bright red tubular flowers throughout summer.

Oriental bittersweet (Celastrus orbiculatus) Vine with bright yellow seed-pods opening to reveal orange berries in fall. Instead plant the native species, C. scandens.

Hardy ageratum (Eupatorium coelestinum) Perennial with blue flowers in late summer.

Gooseneck loosestrife (Lysimachia clethroides) Perennial with white flowers throughout much of summer.

Sundrops (Oenothera fruticosa) Perennial with yellow flowers in late spring and early summer.

Star-of-Bethlehem (Ornithogalum umbellatum) Bulb with clusters of white flowers in spring.

Flowering raspberry (Rubus odoratus) Shrub with magenta flowers in summer.

Plants grow in a wide variety of soils—from Alaskan tundra to Louisiana swamps, Colorado mountains, and New Jersey beaches. However, most individual plants do well only in particular types of soil. Thus, a crucial first step in designing a low-maintenance garden is to evaluate your soil and the kinds of plants that grow best in it.

Clay and sand represent two extreme soil conditions. Clay soil consists of tiny, thin particles packed together so tightly that water has difficulty seeping through. Dense and heavy clay tends to block the spread of roots and may ultimately suffocate them. Yet clay soil is usually loaded with nutrients because these have little opportunity to wash away.

Sandy soil contains large, loose-fitting particles that constantly shift. It has many air pockets for water to drain through and ample room for roots to spread. However, in this porous soil nutrients are quickly washed away.

Although you can find suitable plants for clay or sandy soil, you can greatly expand your selection by improving the soil with organic matter. To do this, work plenty of composted leaves and grass clippings, peat moss, aged animal manures, and other organic materials into the garden.

Don't, however, pile on the fertilizers and make the soil too rich; some plants that are easy to care for in soil of average fertility become invasive in highly fertile soil and require more work to keep under control. Your goal is to create soil that drains within an hour after heavy rain, crumbles fairly easily in your hand, and is full of nutrients (see pages 76–79).

Some plants grow too well if given optimum conditions. In wet soils, purple loose-strife spreads so vigorously that it can become pernicious. Talk to gardening neighbors and county cooperative extension staff about plants that are especially good—and bad—choices for your area.

Violets (Viola *spp.*) *are charming for shady spots, but they do spread. In their ideal growing conditions they can become invasive.*

1 *To get a representative sampling of soil, mix trowelfuls of soil from different parts of the garden together. If using a home test kit, put a small amount of soil in a test tube.*

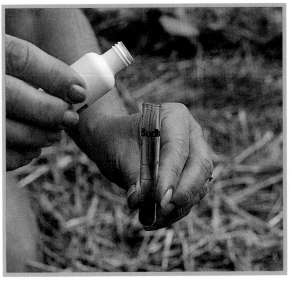

2 *Add the required amount of indicator fluid to the collected soil. Gently shake the test tube, and wait for the contents to settle.*

This fragrant Solomon's-seal (Polygonatum odoratum 'Variegatum') *thrives in acid soil.*

3 *Compare the tube to the test kit's color chart. The more expensive test kits give more accurate information on your soil conditions than very inexpensive kits.*

4 *If your soil's pH is too low, add lime to raise the level. To lower the pH level, work powdered sulfur or wood ashes into the soil.*

Ice plant grows best in alkaline soil, which is prevalent in much of the western United States. It's a popular ground cover in southern California.

Light

When planting short, sun-loving flowers and vegetables, make sure they are not shaded by taller ones. Black-eyed Susans, for example, can block sunlight from reaching low-growing portulacas. Similarly, beets may not receive enough sunshine if their leaves are overshadowed by neighboring tomato plants.

A lovely combination for a shady spot: columbines (Aquilegia spp.) in violet, pink, and white float behind the deep red heart-shaped flowers of wild bleeding-heart (Dicentra eximia).

The lacy flower heads of lily leek (Allium moly) and hot-colored rock rose (Cistus crispus) put on a lively summer show in a sun-drenched informal garden.

All plants need a certain amount of light to grow, so you must carefully evaluate how much light your site receives, with attention to variations in light with the time of day and season. To get an accurate reading, check your growing area in early morning, around noon, and toward evening in spring, summer, and fall.

Recognize light patterns throughout the growing season. Suppose, for example, you add charming yellow-flowered marsh marigolds to your garden in spring. Knowing these gems require moisture and shade, you place them in a dim spot by a pond. Yet during the summer, when the sun is higher in the sky, a place that was shaded in early spring could be exposed to baking sun. The marsh marigold might die because it was planted where light conditions were suitable for only part of the year.

You can, however, alter the light in your garden and broaden your plant selection possibilities. To increase light in wooded areas, lop off the lower limbs of trees or thin out shrubs. Lighten the tree canopy by removing selected higher branches. As a last resort, trees can be cut down, so sun-loving plants get the amount of light they need.

To reflect additional light into the garden area, paint nearby buildings white or use brilliant white pebbles to pave a terrace or garden path.

To decrease the amount of light, build trellises or lath houses (see page 32) to shade plants sensitive to hot sun. Or plant a hedge or border of tall shrubs or small trees to gain shade and privacy (see the encyclopedia beginning on page 98 for suggestions).

Moisture

*T*he moisture content of the soil on your property greatly affects the design of your low-maintenance garden. Examine your proposed garden site as it naturally exists. Is it typically dry or wet? Once you've determined your soil moisture conditions, you can either amend the soil or choose plants that flourish in the sort of wet or dry soil present in your garden.

Most plants thrive in reasonably well-drained soil. Plants that require little care, such as artemisia, will not only thrive, but will also be able to weather short-term changes in moisture content.

If your soil is excessively wet or dry, and you elect to use plants naturally suited to either situation rather than to amend your soil, you need to plan defensive measures to save your plants in the event of unexpected changes in the amount of moisture present in the soil.

If your garden is usually dry and you decide to grow drought-tolerant plants, you may want to ensure continued good drainage in the proposed garden site before you start planting. Good drainage will prevent unusually heavy downpours or extended spells of wet weather from creating lingering puddles that could drown your plants. You can improve drainage by building raised beds on top of the existing soil, by installing underground drainage pipes or tiles, or by regrading the area to create a slope that will allow water to drain away. (See pages 32–40 and 84–86 for more information about solving drainage problems.)

If your proposed garden area is generally moist, be prepared to keep it watered in dry weather. The garden should be close to a water source, so that during a drought you can sprinkle the spot daily by hand or with a soaker hose.

Astilbes and irises like moist soil and thrive in the damp environs next to a pond or stream.

Hardiness and Climate

Plants for Cool Climates

The following plants can survive winter temperatures as low as –40°F:

Monkshood
(Aconitum napellus)
Perennial with rich violet-blue flowers.

Canada wild ginger
(Asarum canadense)
Ground cover with green heart-shaped leaves.

Siberian dogwood
(Cornus alba 'Sibirica')
Native shrub with vivid coral red bark.

Garden peony
(Paeonia lactiflora 'Festiva Maxima')
Perennial with fragrant, white, double flowers.

Iceland poppy
(Papaver nudicaule)
Perennial with fragrant flowers in many colors.

Chokecherry
(Prunus virginiana 'Shubert')
Native tree with foliage that turns red in summer; purple fruit used for making jelly.

Siberian squill
(Scilla siberica)
Bulb with brilliant blue flowers in spring.

Appalachian tea
(Viburnum cassinoides)
Shrub with red fall foliage and multicolored berries.

With fewer pest and disease problems than found in warmer climates, many annuals perform beautifully in the North.

When gardeners talk about hardiness and climate, they are referring to three weather factors: temperature, humidity, and snowfall. Although rain is certainly a weather component, its absence can be amended by watering and its excess can be alleviated by adding ditches and drainage mechanisms.

There is little, however, that a gardener can do about the degree of heat or cold, the amount of moisture in the air, or how much snow falls on the garden.

When choosing plants for your garden you must take into account these existing conditions.

A low-maintenance garden should contain plants that can adapt to both the lowest and highest temperatures likely to occur in the garden. For too many years, garden books and mail-order nursery catalogues have concentrated on a plant's tolerance of winter cold in defining hardiness. Indeed, the U.S. Department of Agriculture publishes a plant hardiness

Southern gardens have their own special grace. In spring this elegant courtyard garden shimmers with the soft color of easy-care white azaleas and a lovely ornamental cherry tree.

Warm-Climate Plants
These plants will not survive when temperatures drop below 5°F:

Kiwi berry
(Actinidia chinensis)
Handsome vine with fragrant flowers and edible fruit.

Lily-of-the-Nile
(Agapanthus orientalis)
Bulb with blue or white flowers in summer.

Camellia
(C. japonica)
Small tree with glossy dark green leaves and large beautiful flowers.

California lilac
(Ceanothus × delilianus)
Hybrid shrub with pale or deep blue flowers.

White rock rose
(Cistus × hybridus)
A bushy shrub with white flowers throughout summer.

Crape myrtle
(Lagerstroemia indica)
Small native tree with lovely summer flowers in colors from whites to purples.

Scarlet sage
(Salvia splendens)
Perennial in southern U.S. with brilliant red flowers; grown as annual elsewhere.

zone map that shows the average minimum temperature in regions across the country (see page 127). Summer heat, however, can be equally lethal to many plants, as southern gardeners know only too well.

Humidity is another weather factor that bedevils many gardeners. It seems almost cruel that high humidity can exist hand in hand with drought, and yet this occurs frequently in southeastern gardens. If sultry heat is common in your area, be warned that many plants that can tolerate temperature extremes will rot in humid conditions.

Gorgeous perennials such as phlox, obedient plant *(Physostegia virginiana)*, and lungwort *(Pulmonaria* spp.*)*, which are otherwise low in maintenance, will not grow well in excessively humid areas. Even some invasive plants, such as carpet bugleweed *(Ajuga* spp.*)*, melt in muggy summer weather. Not surprisingly, two

southeastern natives—blue false indigo *(Baptisia australis)* and golden star *(Chrysogonum virginianum)*—have no problems with such weather.

Finally, snowfall can significantly affect the survival of plants. Snow acts as an insulating blanket, protecting plants that are normally damaged by sub-freezing temperatures. If you live in a very cold area but have a constant winter snow cover, you can probably grow a larger selection of plants than gardeners who live in areas that are somewhat warmer but without significant snowfall.

If you have questions about whether a plant is suitable for your area, call your local USDA county cooperative extension agent. In addition, check with neighbors and local gardening friends to find out which plants grow best for them.

Plant Groupings

**TROUBLESHOOTING
TIP**

Choose disease-resistant varieties when planting in drifts or large groups of one kind of plant. If you are unsure if a plant is suitable for your garden, just plant one or two specimens initially. If they survive, continue to incorporate many more in your garden design.

*T*he old saying that opposites attract doesn't apply to growing low-maintenance plants. One of the keys to reducing your involvement in a beautiful easy-care garden is to group plants with similar needs.

Water-loving plants should be placed together in a moist setting. If you don't have a wet location, make sure that these kinds of plants are close to water sources such as faucets or hoses, so you can water them easily. Even better, from a low-maintenance point of view, avoid growing plants that need a lot of water if you don't have a constantly moist area.

Similarly, try to place plants that prefer dry conditions in well-drained areas. Drought-tolerant plants such as honey locust, lemon bottlebrush, and golden marguerite can be planted farthest from the house because they do not need to be near water sources.

Another old saying—the one about beauty being skin-deep—*does* apply to low-maintenance gardens. When planning your design scheme, first group plants by their basic growth characteristics and needs rather than by their outward appearances. Consider the matter of appearance only at the end, when other requirements have been met.

In planning a low-maintenance garden—or any garden, for that matter—put all the sun lovers together on one list, shade plants on another, and so forth. Next, break down these plant lists by moisture requirements. On the sun list, for example, set up three subheadings: tolerates drought, normal moisture, needs lots of water. If you don't have a spot on your property that is more or less constantly wet, don't even consider plants in the last category.

The purpose of creating these lists and winnowing them down is to ensure that each group of plants is growing under optimal conditions in your garden.

One of the great challenges in grouping ornamental plants is designing an all-season border. This idea of a garden with flowers from spring to fall has gained prominence in recent years because many homeowners have relatively small plots of land and want to pack as many plants as possible into their gardens.

Unless you have spectacular growing conditions, having a border that is both loaded with flowers from spring to fall and easy to maintain is, in all probability, not possible. With careful planning, however, you *can* have something of interest throughout the growing season in your low-maintenance garden. A simple way to plan multiseason color is to include some spring bulbs and a flowering shrub with good-looking leaves and fall color. The bulbs will give you color in early spring, and the shrub will provide a changing focal point for the garden.

In other parts of your border you can overplant to achieve color during more than one season. Overplanting means planting shallow-rooted plants on top of those buried deeper in the ground. For example, shallow-rooted bulbs such as crocuses can be planted above deeper-rooted lily bulbs. While both have similar growth requirements, the crocus flowers in late winter and then goes dormant. Later, the narrow stems of the lilies shoot up through the middle of the crocus planting and carry blooms in summer. Another classic overplanting technique is to plant annuals among, around, and on top of spring bulbs. As the bulb foliage matures and the plants go dormant, the annuals spread and provide summer color.

If overplanting to achieve an all-season border is too much work and planning for you, concentrate on more easily constructed seasonal gardens. You might plant spring bloomers in one part of your property, create a great summer border in another section, and save a third plot for fall flowers.

Lawns and Ground Covers

*L*ush, smooth, weed-free green lawns don't occur naturally. The invention and mass production of the mechanical lawn mower in the late nineteenth century gave gardeners the false hope that such an impossible dream was easily within their reach. It quickly became apparent that while a mowing machine could cut the grass, it could not keep away weeds or insects, and it certainly didn't guarantee that the grass would get adequate moisture.

A century after the appearance of the lawn mower, the lawn-care industry boomed. This is certainly a case of a service arising to meet a definite need.

The only easy way to have a lush, velvety green low-maintenance lawn is to hire a firm to care for it.

Depending on the amount they charge and what you are willing to pay, the firm will regularly mow, fertilize, and apply pesticides to maintain a gorgeous stretch of greenery for you.

Neat expanses of perfect grass do not occur in nature. In fact, to achieve the ideal lawn you have to work *against* nature. The traditional manicured bluegrass sward has required regular applications of fertilizers, herbicides, and pesticides. But some of these products have proven harmful to the environment. Diazinon, for example, once widely used as an animal deterrent, is so highly toxic to birds that its use is illegal on sod farms and golf courses. Weed killers can also be dangerous on lawns, particularly when they

Ground Covers Under Shrubs

Lawn grass seldom flourishes under shrubs. To reduce watering, mowing, and fertilizing chores, plant some of these ground covers instead:

Goutweed (Aegopodium podagraria *'Variegatum')*, *with its striking green and white foliage, is an invasive plant but perfect for areas where nothing else will grow. If you're looking for a slow-spreading ground cover, try Canada wild ginger (Asarum canadense). This native plant has green, heart-shaped leaves. Another invasive plant, but one that is easier to contain than goutweed, is yellow archangel*

(Lamiastrum galeobdolon). *It has variegated leaves and yellow flowers in spring. Sweet woodruff* (Galium odoratum) *has warm green foliage and tiny white flowers in spring. The ubiquitous Japanese pachysandra* (P. terminalis) *is popular as a mostly evergreen ground cover with white flowers in spring. Another quickly spreading ground cover is periwinkle* (Vinca minor). *Its lovely blue-violet flowers appear in spring; unique cultivars have white flowers* ('Alba') *and variegated foliage* ('Variegata').

Lawns and Ground Covers CONTINUED

Tall fescue (Festuca arundi-nacea) *is a good lawn grass for shade.*

are indiscriminately applied and wipe out nearby ornamental plants.

If you choose not to use pesticides, you can simply mow the lawn once a week and let nature take its course. Some weeds are actually beneficial; clover, for example, adds nitrogen to the soil. Dandelions have cheerful yellow flowers and nutritious edible leaves. Plantains and wild strawberries can be appreciated for their green foliage.

The Lawn Institute, in cooperation with the American Seed Trade Association, counsels home-owners not to despair if they're looking for an unde-manding but attractive swath of green. The institute offers free lawn-care brochures covering such useful topics as How to Select the Best Grass Seed for Northern (or Southern) Lawns, Home Lawn-Care Programs That Work, How to Read a Seed Label to

Determine Quality, and What You Need to Know about Home-Lawn Fertilizers.

In addition, the institute regularly reviews and updates a listing of high-quality turf grass. It has also developed a new climatic zone map with recommen-dations by zone of turf grass blends and mixtures by percentages. This publication includes recommenda-tions for sunny areas, shaded areas, low-maintenance areas, and heavy-traffic areas.

Using the free guidelines (in many cases developed for particular areas of the country) provided by the Lawn Institute, you should be able to have a reason-ably attractive lawn. (See page 129 for the institute's address.) In addition, you can further reduce lawn-maintenance chores by implementing the design tips shown in the photos to the right and those discussed on page 22.

1 *Ground covers often grow better than lawn under trees and shrubs. First prepare the soil, taking care not to damage the shallow roots.*

2 *Set ground-cover plants at the recommended spacing distance, staggering plants to provide even coverage of the ground.*

3 *Water well to settle the plants into the soil. Keep the soil evenly moist but not soggy for a week or two as the plants become established.*

Instead of battling the lawn mower to trim the grass on a slope, plant ornamental grasses and low-maintenance perennials on the hillside. This California garden includes reed grass (Calamagrostis), *lavender* (Lavandula spp.), *and the spires of tower of jewels* (Echium wildpretii).

One way to reduce the time required to maintain a lawn is to group shrubs and trees in borders or island beds instead of planting them as individual specimens. To eliminate laborious hand trimming of grass along the edge of the garden, edge with flat stones or bricks that allow the lawn mower wheel to roll on the edging.

Another low-maintenance option for a slope is to plant it with ground covers. The hill to the right of the steps of this garden is carpeted with cranesbill (Geranium macrorrhizum 'Bevan's Variety').

Lawns and Ground Covers CONTINUED

There are some areas, such as the ground under a shallow-rooted maple tree, where grass will not grow, no matter how much tender loving care you provide. On other sites, such as steep slopes, it is simply too much work to maintain grass. These places are perfect candidates for ground covers.

Ground covers are excellent grass substitutes because they don't need to be mowed, require little if any fertilizer or pesticide, and often provide extra interest with flowers or variegated foliage. In a land-scaped setting, ground covers are an attractive design element, particularly when used visually to connect islands of shrubs.

Shade-tolerant ground covers are perfect for dim spots, especially those punctuated by tree or shrub roots. The step-by-step photographs on page 20 illus-trate how to plant ground covers under a shrub.

When designing with ground covers, take note of their density and rate of spread in addition to their flowers and foliage. Gingers *(Asarum spp.)*, for example, form thick carpets in the shade; while they may smother potential weeds, the plants are slow to spread. Conversely, periwinkle *(Vinca spp.)*, a creeping vine that spreads quickly by sending out run-ners, often leaves open spaces, where tree seedlings and weeds can sprout.

Take care when planting fast-spreading, invasive ground covers. Choose plants that are shallow-rooted, such as carpet bugleweed *(Ajuga reptans)*. As further protection against undesirable spreading, you can install underground plastic or metal barriers to a depth of up to 1 foot.

Cool-Season and Warm-Season Lawns for Hot Climates

To keep lawns green throughout the year, southern homeowners over-seed bermudagrass (Cynodon dactylon) with improved perennial ryegrass (Lolium perenne). The bermudagrass (pictured at left) thrives in hot weather and goes dor-mant in cool; the ryegrass reacts in an opposite manner. Depending on how green you want your winter lawn, seed the perennial ryegrass in September at a rate of 3 to 8 pounds per 1,000 square feet. The only equipment you will need is a seed or fer-tilizer spreader. Should the perennial ryegrass persist when warm weather returns, just mow closely to the ground and withhold watering. These two mea-sures will encourage the bermudagrass to take over.

Shrub Borders

For a handsome bed or border that requires less work than a conventional flower garden, plant shrubs and small trees. Azaleas bring spring color to this garden, and dwarf conifers add year-round texture.

For well over a century, most American gardeners have viewed shrubs as plants to be placed as specimens (focal points) in lawns or grouped about the foundation of a house. Foundation plantings have generally consisted of rhododendrons, azaleas, and yews or other needled evergreens sheared into cones or mounds. The rhododendrons and azaleas provide a burst of color, often in spring, and then remain green for the rest of the garden season, or even year-round.

In recent years sophisticated gardeners have recognized the value of shrubs in other areas, particularly flower borders. Shrubs and small trees add large, long-lasting architectural elements to borders and can provide effective, easy-care backgrounds for the flowers of annuals, bulbs, and perennials. In windy locations shrubs are also valuable as windbreaks (as shown in the step-by-step photo sequence on page 43).

Shrubs are woody plants. Unlike perennials, which die back to the ground in winter, shrubs leave part of their tough stems above ground in cold months. Some shrubs, such as rhododendrons, are evergreen and retain their leaves throughout winter. Others, such as most azaleas, are deciduous; that is, they lose their foliage during winter and then send out new leaves when warm weather returns.

Recognize the difference between evergreen and deciduous shrubs when incorporating them into your garden. If you opt for a deciduous shrub, consider how it will look in winter when it is "naked." Some low-maintenance shrubs, such as Tatarian dogwood

Shrub Borders CONTINUED

Mixed borders of shrubs, small trees, and perennials are interesting all year and less work than gardens of herbaceous perennials. The garden pictured on this page contains several azaleas, including the unusual violet blossoms of Rhododendron *'Blue Bird', along with Lawson false cypress* (Chamaecyparis lawsoniana) *and tall Stewartia* (Stewartia monadelpha *'Nana'*). Viburnums *(detail, above) are durable, easy-care shrubs with clusters of white (or yellowish or greenish) flowers.*

(Cornus alba 'Sibirica'*)* and redosier dogwood *(C. sericea),* have colored stems in interesting configurations. Others, such as burning bush *(Euonymus alata* 'Compacta'*),* have textured bark.

Though all shrubs are "clothed" with foliage in spring, not all are simultaneously decorated with flowers. To increase the attractiveness of your garden, include some low-maintenance, summer-flowering shrubs in your design. Three exceptionally low-maintenance native plants that add colorful touches are the plum-leaved azalea *(Rhododendron prunifolium),* rosebay rhododendron *(R. maximum),* and oakleaf hydrangea *(H. quercifolia).* Oakleaf hydrangea, which thrives in sun or shade, provides lovely large flowers and an extra garden bonus—its handsome foliage turns red in the fall.

Because shrubs come in all sizes, horticulturists often have a hard time distinguishing between a large shrub and a small tree. Before you choose a shrub or a small tree for your border, determine the mature size of the plant, and consider how the plant will fit into the overall garden when it reaches adult size.

Small shrubs, such as dwarf fothergilla *(F. gardenii* 'Blue Mist'*),* are perfect for compact garden areas. Large borders, on the other hand, can easily handle—and often require—the dramatic presence of a large shrub such as butterfly bush *(Buddleia davidii),* which produces a magnificent fountain of flowers from midsummer until frost.

Though you may have to wait several years before a newly planted shrub reaches its full size, take its ultimate height into account when planning your border. While it's relatively easy to move flowers, relocating an inappropriately placed shrub is definitely not a low-maintenance task!

1 The first step in planting a bed or border of mixed shrubs is to prepare the soil. If you are creating a new garden, first remove the sod. Then loosen the soil and work in 2 inches of compost.

2 Edge the bed with boulders, bricks, or field-stone. Roll—do not lift—large rocks into place. This physical barrier will help prevent the lawn grass from spreading into the garden.

3 Before digging any holes, set out the plants in their containers to find the best arrangement and correct spacing. Step back and take a look at your design; then adjust plants as necessary.

4 If plants have been in their containers all summer, trim roots that have grown through the drainage holes. If you buy plants with overgrown roots, check to make sure they are healthy.

5 Dig a generous-sized hole that is wider than the plant's rootball. Loosen the soil in the bottom and sides of the hole, set in the plant, and firm soil around the roots.

6 Each shrub should sit at the same depth it was growing in the container. Repeat the planting procedure until all the shrubs are in the ground; then water the plants well.

Foliage

Shrubs with Colored and Variegated Foliage

Foliage colors on these easy-care shrubs are as pleasing in the garden as any flowers.

Japanese maple
(Acer palmatum *'Bloodgood'*)
Beautiful red leaves throughout summer.

Gold-dust tree
(Aucuba japonica *'Variegata'*)
Bright green leaves splotched with yellow; hardy only to zone 7.

Smoke tree
(Cotinus coggygria *'Royal Purple'*)
Rich purple foliage.

Daphne
(D. × burkwoodii *'Carol Mackie'*)
Dark green leaves edged with a creamy band.

Wintercreeper
(Euonymus fortunei *'Gracilis'*)
Variegated leaves with white, yellow, or pink margins.

Variegated bigleaf hydrangea
(H. macrophylla *'Variegata'*)
Toothed green leaves edged in white or cream.

Creeping juniper
(Juniperus horizontalis *'Wiltonii'*)
Intense silver-blue foliage.

*T*o open up the most design opportunities, consider foliage as well as flowers and overall plant form when designing the garden. Foliage can play an especially important role in low-maintenance gardens, since foliage plants generally require less maintenance than flowering plants. Carefully designed gardens that feature leaf color, form, and texture create a pleasing picture even when no flowers are in bloom.

American gardeners can look to our British counterparts for superb examples of incorporating foliage into design schemes to create beautiful results. Visit major British gardens today and you will see stunning backdrops of shrubs and trees covered with deep purple leaves. The purple-leaved plants may be interlaced with plants decked with variegated foliage or others bearing leaves splashed with white or gray or dotted with golden yellow. The addition of some flowering annuals, bulbs, and perennials complements the array of leaf colors and textures.

In their mixed borders, many British gardeners like to incorporate plants that have both colorful flowers and attractive foliage. The shade-loving Siberian bugloss *(Brunnera macrophylla)*, for example, is covered in spring with sky blue flowers that resemble forget-me-nots. During the remainder of the garden year this easy-to-grow perennial features large, dark green leaves.

Designing with foliage is a great way to create a beautiful garden without the work of pinching and deadheading that flowers require. Foliage plants stay tidy without a lot of fussing.

This formal elegance is achieved with easy-care foliage plants. Deep burgundy beefsteak plant (Iresine herbstii) and Joseph's-coat or copperleaf (Alternanthera) are featured players in this warm-climate garden.

Coleus offers a broad choice of foliage colors and patterns, especially if you grow it from seed.

This striking lily-of-the-valley (Convallaria majalis 'Variegata') has rich green leaves striped with ivory.

A subtle composition of small foliage plants looks exquisite in a postage-stamp-size garden. This planting demonstrates an effective combination of leaf textures and colorations.

The arresting foliage of the annual Joseph's-coat (Amaranthus tricolor) is a show-stopper.

When choosing foliage plants, consider not only their ease of care, but also their ability to resist disease and insects. Be sure, too, that the plants are hardy in your particular area.

Two plants that are often attractively paired in American shade gardens are hostas and ferns. The bold, sculptural foliage of the hostas offers a lovely contrast to the light and airy ferns. Some native flowering plants can also be used to create pleasing foliage combinations. One favorite perennial is the sun-loving Moonbeam coreopsis, whose pale yellow flowers cover a small mass of thin, wiry stems; its fine-textured foliage blends well with the more solid, scalloped leaf clumps of coralbells *(Heuchera sanguinea)*. While both plants flower for long periods, their foliage contrasts provide continued garden interest when the blooms peter out.

To use plant foliage as a design element in a low-maintenance garden, begin by choosing shrubs and trees with colorful leaves to incorporate into the backdrop of your border. Then choose blooming plants—annuals, bulbs, and perennials—on the basis of their flower color as well as their foliage form and texture. Consider, too, if there are variegated species of any of your favorite plants, and see if these can be worked into your design scheme.

Vegetables

Try planting herbs in your vegetable garden to repel insect pests instead of using pesticides. For example, some people believe that basil deters flies and mosquitoes, that chives discourage aphids and Japanese beetles, that rosemary repels bean beetles, and that sage chases away cabbage moths. Even if the herbs don't entirely live up to their reputation, they still look pretty in the garden.

Poor soil and lack of sun need not be deterrents in designing a low-maintenance ornamental garden, but they can be fatal conditions for a vegetable garden. Most vegetables need rich, fertile, well-drained soil, and unless you plan to concentrate on leafy greens, your garden should have at least six full hours of direct sun (preferably more) every day.

To check the fertility of your garden plot, take a soil sample to your local county cooperative extension agent and have it analyzed. Follow the recommendations in the test report for improving the soil. Working in plenty of compost is one of the best ways to enrich and maintain soil. Organic mulches will add organic material to the soil as they break down. A classic

work-saving way to grow vegetables, developed by gardener Ruth Stout in the 1960s, is the permanent-mulch garden. Stout kept her garden covered with 1 foot of loose mulch all year. To plant she simply pulled the mulch aside, put in seeds or plants, then replaced the mulch as the plants grew. Over the years she developed excellent soil and had superior harvests without digging or weeding. This permanent-mulch technique is illustrated in the step-by-step photographs on page 29.

If your soil does not drain well, a raised bed may be the simplest way to create a growing area. Use rocks or lumber to build retaining walls, then fill the enclosed area with fertile, humusy, well-drained soil. (See the step-by-step photographs of constructing raised beds on page 40.)

A salad garden planted in neat rows or blocks can be ornamental in its own right, as well as edible. Mulching reduces maintenance. This elegant raised bed includes romaine lettuce, several kinds of leaf lettuce, carrots (foreground) and cress (next to flowers).

1 *A permanent-mulch garden stays covered with mulch all year. When it is time to plant, simply pull the mulch aside and prepare the planting area of the soil below.*

2 *Plant seeds (like the beans shown here) or place vegetables at or close to the recommended spacing distance and depth; then be sure to water them well.*

3 *When seeded plants are a few inches tall, thin them as necessary. Then replace the mulch, tucking it around the base of each plant. The garden should stay weed-free all season long.*

Build several small vegetable gardens in this manner rather than one large one. A small size lets you walk around the garden to tend to it or pick vegetables; you do not compact the soil by stepping in.

With sun and soil conditions met, the next step is to count the people you intend to feed with the harvest from your garden. Low-maintenance gardeners have to be a bit selfish: unless you want to spend extra time on planting, maintenance, and harvesting, you can't share your bounty with friends.

Your goal should be to have the smallest possible garden that will yield the maximum harvest. Eliminate sprawling plants, such as pumpkins, that take up space. Try to include leafy greens and cut-and-come-again crops such as broccoli, which continues to pro-duce side heads after the main head has been cut. You may have to eliminate vegetables such as potatoes and winter squash, which are only harvested once after a long growing season.

To increase productivity, use succession planting to get several harvests from one space. For example, plant early cool-growing crops such as lettuce, green onions, and radishes; when these are harvested and the ground has warmed, put in tomatoes, peppers, or other warm-weather crops.

Paths

Paths are important structural elements in a garden or landscape. A well-designed path ties the garden together and leads you from one section to another.

A designer purely interested in aesthetics makes paths fit the beauty of the setting. Low-maintenance gardeners, however, take a slightly different approach: they view paths as camouflage devices, covering up areas where it is difficult to grow plants.

To try this approach, single out difficult-to-maintain sites on your property. Next, determine if it's possible to lay paths to cover over these problem spots and eliminate garden work. As a bonus, paths add color (red brick, white pebbles, or blue slate, for example) and form to your property.

Paths can be made of many different materials for a wide range of effects. As shown in the photos below, brick patterns can be attractive features in their own right. Although a brick path is time-consuming and fairly expensive to construct, once it's built it requires very little maintenance.

If you opt for a simpler path of pebbles or wood chips, lay heavy black plastic in the pathways to suppress weeds before spreading the path material. Keep invasive and self-seeding plants away from the path's edges, or they may turn your neat walkway into a jungle. Moss, for example, often spreads uninvited along damp, shaded paths. If this occurs, clean the path with a moss-inhibitor once or twice a year.

Paths provide a lovely garden setting for small plants that will not overrun them. Uncover small spaces in a walkway by removing a few bricks or flagstones. Fill the resulting pockets with good soil, and plant noninvasive shallow-rooted flowers or herbs right in the path. Herbs are particularly popular among gardeners who love a fragrant garden. As the herbs are stepped on, they release their pungent aromas. Popular herbs to plant along a path include creeping chamomile *(Chamaemelum nobile)* and various thymes *(Thymus spp.)*.

A brick path in a stack pattern draws the eye toward the destination.

A simple running bond pattern of bricks is nicely dressed up with curved and circular accents.

A diagonal herringbone brick path becomes especially decorative with an additional pattern of contrasting light-colored bricks.

Moss growing between the bricks gives this path a soft-edged antique look. Bricks are laid in a basket weave pattern.

Salvaged bricks laid in a fan pattern pave a curved path that winds between garden areas.

1 *The first step to building a path is to measure and lay out where it will go. Lay out the length of the path with strong cord stretched between stakes at each end.*

2 *Excavate a few inches of soil from the path, so that it will be level with the surrounding area when completed. Use a carpenter's level to check for evenness if the path is not on a slope.*

3 *Rake the soil to get a smooth surface. If the soil is still somewhat uneven or lumpy, rake again in a direction 90 degrees opposite to the first raking.*

4 *Adjust the stretched cords so that they run parallel to each other. Place wooden boards at each end of the path as edgers to contain the paving material.*

5 *Line the path with sturdy black plastic sheeting to thwart weeds. Install edgings of wood, brick, or stone along the sides of the path to hold the paving material in place.*

6 *Spread bluestone (shown here), gravel, or pebbles in the path and rake smooth. You can also pave with wood chips, but they will need to be replaced each year.*

Hot and Dry Conditions

Many native and naturalized plants thrive in the dry heat of the Southwest, but plants in other places may have a hard time with such weather. A hot drought is often followed by excessive rain and high humidity. Plants that survive in the hot, dry period often rot or drown when the rains arrive.

Gardeners in areas that suffer periodic, rather than constant, dry heat must employ a battery of defenses to ensure that their beds are both attractive and low in maintenance. Many of these measures are also helpful for southwestern gardeners.

Silver-leaved plants such as lamb's-ears (Stachys byzan-tina) are often good choices for hot, dry conditions. Lavender (Lavandula spp.), seen at left behind the lamb's-ears, also likes plenty of sun and well-drained soil.

▼ Improving the Garden Site

As discussed earlier, location is a key factor in garden design. Light, grading, drainage patterns, and soil composition must all be evaluated.

Some plants, such as snow-in-summer *(Cerastium tomentosum)* and hardy geraniums, need to be shielded from the burning rays of dry summer sun, especially in southern gardens. Although these two plants prefer full sun in the North, they grow better with some shade in warmer climates. Even with continuous watering, moisture evaporates quickly in the intense sun.

When dry heat bakes out soil moisture it causes an increase in transpiration from leaves. Transpiration occurs when plants draw moisture from the soil through their roots and then "sweat" it out through their leaves to cool off. Up to 120 gallons of water can be transpired through a pecan tree in a day. Trees, especially those with shallow roots, are widely believed to use so much water that the soil is left too dry for smaller plants nearby. But some researchers have found that trees may act as hydraulic pumps in dry areas and actually flush water from their roots into the soil at night.

Thus, a shaded site might be ideal for gardening during dry heat. If a suitable shady location is not available, you can reduce potential water loss by constructing a lath house to shield heat-sensitive plants. This simple structure is built of wood strips (laths); light gently filters through its walls and ceiling. A lath house is, in effect, a screened porch for your plants and can be a stunning design element. It also makes a good summer home for houseplants.

Consider the grade, or slope, of your property when placing drought-resistant plants in your garden. If your property is flat, you can create your own grade

1 *Drought-tolerant annuals provide color with a minimum of maintenance where summers are hot and dry. Prepare the soil for planting, working in lots of compost to help hold moisture.*

2 *If you are using container-grown plants, set them out in your prepared garden site in their pots to determine the best arrangement before you start to dig.*

3 *Dig a planting hole big enough to comfortably hold the rootball, slide the plant from its pot, and position it in the hole. The plant should sit at the same depth it was growing in the container.*

4 *If the depth of the plant is correct, firm the soil around the rootball. When all plants are in place, water well.*

5 *Spread gravel around the plants to keep down weeds and provide a base for a decorative maintenance-free stone mulch.*

6 *Set the larger stones into position to create an attractive mulch. Leave some space between stones and around bases of plants to let in water.*

Hot and Dry Conditions CONTINUED

**TROUBLESHOOTING
TIP**

*In many areas of the
country, dry summers are
preceded by wet winters or
rainy springs. Be sure that
the perennials or shrubs you
choose for these areas can
tolerate early-season moisture as well as summer
drought.*

to guide water flow. Place plants that need more water
at the bottom of the slope, where moisture collects,
and drought-tolerant species farther up the hill, where
drainage will be faster.

You can also improve drainage by installing underground drainage pipes or tiles to direct water to plants
that most require it. These hidden pipes provide moisture to plants without detracting from the garden's
appearance.

If you see that water drains almost instantly from a
proposed garden area, you probably have sandy soil.
To grow plants other than seashore plants, you will
need to amend the soil with clay and organic matter,
so that it retains moisture better.

All of these site-improvement measures will make
your garden a low-maintenance one, but they may be
seen as too much preparatory work. The solution is
simple: reduce the size of the planting area. In gardening, this is known as hardscaping your property.

If trying to maintain a green lawn, for example, is
fast becoming an exercise in futility, install a patio or
terrace and surround it with a drought-tolerant
ground cover. Or create wide, attractive walkways
using bricks, stones, or pavement. Plant short, low-
maintenance shrubs along the border of the walk, and
within the walkway, leave small rectangular or circular dirt areas for decorative drought-resistant plants
such as thyme *(Thymus vulgaris)*.

If even small spaces appear too difficult to plant in,
consider creating a container garden. This low-maintenance practice is ideally suited to hot and dry conditions because the containers (plastic, not terra-cotta,
which leaks moisture) limit the watering area and can
be moved to fit any design. Watering plants will be
even less time-consuming if you group containers in
one spot.

▼ Providing Moisture

Once you've properly designed your garden site, you
can take three additional steps to ensure adequate
moisture for your plants: adding polymers, applying
mulch, and installing drip-irrigation systems.

Popularly known as water-absorbing polymers, the
recently developed cross-linked polyacrylamides aid
gardening in dry areas. The polymers consist of small
pebblelike particles that are incorporated into dry soil,
which is then heavily watered. The crystals expand
into gelatinous material that captures and holds the
water. The crystals remain filled with water for long
periods of time.

The polymers are powerful water suitcases: 1 ounce
of dry material can store up to 3 gallons of water. This
water then slowly dampens nearby plant roots.
Because the crystals can swell dramatically when
watered, be careful when adding polymers; in large
volumes, the swelling crystals may push plants out of
the soil. Although effective water retainers, polymers
have a drawback: they are made from natural gas, a
nonrenewable resource.

Mulching, another method used to help soil retain
moisture, has become an increasingly popular garden
technique. While there are many kinds of mulches,
from straw and wood chips to plastics and pebbles,
low-maintenance gardeners in hot, dry areas will
probably do best with organic materials. These materials provide a protective blanket that helps slow the
evaporation of soil moisture and keeps roots cooler.
They also enrich the soil as they decompose (thus
increasing its water-retaining capacity).

Soaker hoses and other drip-irrigation systems
allow you to water the garden with minimal labor and
water. To buy and install a drip-irrigation system does
require an initial investment of time and money, but

1 *Mulch is one of a gardener's greatest work savers. This page shows four mulch options. Wood chips, shown in this photo, should be spread 3 inches deep.*

2 *Leaves are another excellent mulch, available free of charge if you have trees on your property. Spread the shredded leaves 2 inches deep.*

TIMESAVING TIP

Gardeners coping with hot, dry conditions and full sun should choose buffalo grass for their lawns. It will survive extreme drought, has low soil fertility requirements, and will not grow higher than 5 inches when left unmowed.

3 *Cocoa bean hulls make a very attractive mulch, but they are expensive for large gardens. The hulls smell like chocolate. Spread them 2 inches deep.*

4 *A stone mulch is time-consuming to lay in place, but helps retain heat for tender plants on chilly nights. Stone mulches should be about 2 inches thick.*

Hot and Dry Conditions CONTINUED

this is offset by the savings of hours spent manually watering. (See pages 84–86 for more information on watering your garden.)

▼ Choosing Plants Carefully

Many dry gardens are also subject to rainy spells and periodic storms that dump more than an inch of water at a time, flooding the soil. Some of the most drought-tolerant plants—cacti and succulents, for example—may suffocate or rot from too much moisture. For gardeners who deal with sandy coastal soils or hot, dry midwestern summers, the secret of low-mainte-

nance gardening is to find plants that can tolerate both generally dry conditions and occasional periods of very wet soil.

Luckily, quite a few low-maintenance plants fill the bill. The following plants are all recommended by the U.S. National Arboretum as being exceptionally care-free and beautiful; for additional information, see the encyclopedia section on pages 98–126.

For the perennial garden, you could grow butterfly weed *(Asclepias tuberosa)*, with its bright orange flowers; red-and-yellow blanket flower *(Gaillardia aristata)*; white-flowered evergreen candytuft *(Iberis sempervirens)*; or cushion spurge *(Euphorbia epithymoides)*. Among the annual possibilities, choose rocket larkspur *(Consolida ambigua)*; low-growing, brightly colored rose moss *(Portulaca grandiflora)*; or black-eyed Susan *(Rudbeckia hirta)*.

Ornamental grasses that can tolerate both wet and dry conditions include feather reed grass *(Calamagrostis × acutiflora* 'Stricta'*)* and blue fescue *(Festuca ovina* var. *glauca)*.

Some adaptable shrubs are rockspray cotoneaster *(C. horizontalis)*, sumacs *(Rhus* spp.*)*, rugosa roses *(Rosa rugosa)*, and soapweed *(Yucca glauca)*. Some good woody vines are trumpet creeper *(Campsis radicans)*, trumpet honeysuckle *(Lonicera sempervirens)*, and Boston ivy *(Parthenocissus tricuspidata)*.

Trees to consider include Amur maple *(Acer ginnala)*, hackberry *(Celtis occidentalis)*, and the thornless honey locust *(Gleditsia triacanthos* var. *inermis)*.

The smooth, striped leaves of century plant (Agave americana) *are a bold accent.*

The spine-tipped, overlapping leaves of this unusual agave (A. huachucensis) *resemble those of an artichoke.*

Flat pads of prickly pear cactus (Opuntia) *are studded with gold.*

Slender columns of Cleistocactus strausii *var.* ficii *add height and vertical line to a desert garden.*

Lobivia bruchii *has an interesting starburst pattern of spines.*

Wet Conditions

Gardening in wet conditions has its drawbacks, but it does offer great possibilities for interesting easy-care gardens. Consider, for example, the wilds of the Mississippi Delta in spring. There you can see one of nature's more spectacular shows—millions of Louisiana irises, perhaps the only plant in the world that naturally bears flowers in every color. Reds, blues, yellows, and every possible combination on the color wheel turn the boggy lowlands into a dazzling kaleidoscope. Such a glorious scene is possible only because of the near-swamp conditions.

If you have extremely wet areas on your property, try to turn this condition into an advantage. However, first determine how large an area gets too wet and to what degree—or how often this area remains wet. Understanding these factors will allow you to design a garden that will thrive with a minimum of labor. You can either improve the growing conditions or choose plants that like plenty of moisture.

If your wet area is a relatively small one, you might elect to eliminate it rather than to accommodate it. If the drainage problem is not too severe, you can lighten the soil by working in lots of organic matter, or you can build raised beds on top of the wet ground; fill them with a fertile, well-drained soil mix; and plant in them. The photographs on page 40 illustrate how to create a raised bed.

Drumstick primroses (Primula japonica) *in shades of pink and rose thrive in a damp bog with royal and ostrich ferns.*

Wet Conditions CONTINUED

**TROUBLESHOOTING
TIP**

*If your vegetable garden
becomes a swamp during wet
spells and a raised bed is not
an option, try digging a wide
trench around the garden
border to serve as a catch
basin. Make the slope
sharper on the garden side,
and plant the entire trench
with sod to resist erosion.*

A more labor-intensive solution to altering a site
with poor drainage is to excavate the soil and install
underground drainage tiles or plastic pipes. See page
39 for step-by-step photographs of this procedure.

If your area is too large to alter or is not amenable
to change (a riverbank, for example), you have several
alternatives. The simplest approach is to choose water-
loving plants, such as marsh marigold *(Caltha palus-
tris)* or cardinal flower *(Lobelia cardinalis)*, and if
necessary, to construct raised paths or boardwalks
through the garden so that you can enjoy the garden
from a drier viewpoint.

Another, more elaborate solution is to create a
pond, bog, or water garden in your wet area. This will
probably require some professional help: the land will
have to be carefully sculpted in order to maintain a
continuous supply of water to the area. The added
bonus of having a small pond on your property is that
wildlife naturally gravitates toward wet areas as
drinking places. Numerous birds, such as grackles,
mocking birds, catbirds, cardinals, and nuthatches will
seek out your wet garden. Another approach to
working with an existing wet area is to put in a catch
basin, carefully concealed behind a bank of shrubs, to
store water runoff.

When determining the degree and extent of wet
conditions on your property, you may find that
selected areas are wet some but not all of the time.

Northern gardeners with contoured properties often
experience this scenario.

One example of how periodic wetness can occur is
when freezing temperatures lock moisture in the soil
during the winter and then, with the warmth of
spring, release a steady stream to the lower ground,
which remains frozen. While the spring thaw creates
boglike conditions for only a short time, it can never-
theless drown the roots of many plants. If these conditions exist in your garden, choose moisture-loving
plants and make sure there is a way to keep the area
damp during any summer dry spells.

In other instances, your garden areas may be excessively wet only after heavy rains. In these cases you
clearly need to improve drainage. Or you could consider building a ledge or digging trenches to deflect
runoff water away from the garden.

Finally, there may be some areas on your property
that are consistently damp. From a low-maintenance
point of view, these are the easiest wet conditions to
tackle; just put in lots of moisture-loving plants and
turn the area into a bog garden.

1 To improve poor drainage, install underground pipes or tiles. Dig a trench from the garden to the desired drainage area.

2 The trench should be deep enough for the pipe to lie below the frost line. Spread a few inches of gravel in the bottom and rake smooth.

3 After raking the gravel smooth, lay the PVC drainage pipe on the gravel, with the holes facing downward.

4 Cover the entire drainage pipe with roofing paper in order to seal the joints and protect the pipe from damage.

5 Add 2 or 3 inches more gravel to cover the sealed pipe, then fill up to the surface level with top soil.

6 At the pipe's outlet cover the drainage field with stones or with a moisture-loving ground cover, without blocking the pipe.

Wet Conditions CONTINUED

**EARTH·WISE
TIP**

If your growing area is extremely wet in only one small place, a concentrated soil amendment job may quickly solve the problem. Dig a deep hole—as much as 2 feet—and fill it with a blended mixture of half the original dirt and half compost and other organic matter.

1 *In heavy, slow-draining, but not boggy soil, try a raised bed. To create one in a lawn, first remove the turf. Cut into the sod, push the spade under the sod, and lift it.*

2 *You can make the sides of the raised bed from brick, stone, scrap lumber, or railroad ties. Make sure these materials have not been treated with creosote.*

3 *Secure the corners of a railroad tie bed by installing angle irons on the inside of the wood. This will help hold the raised bed firmly in place.*

4 *Fill the bed with a blend of topsoil and compost. If using garden soil, add builder's sand, vermiculite, or peat moss to lighten the texture. Rake smooth and plant.*

Seashore Conditions

*If your garden is at the
seashore, save yourself the
time and expense of
installing a soaker hose.
Soaker hoses are of little use
in areas with sandy soil
because the water drains
away so fast that it can't
spread to nearby plants or
even encompass the root area
of a single target shrub.
Instead, build up the soil
with organic matter for a few
years to improve the texture.*

Cool breezes are a powerful allure on oceanside
properties, particularly during summer. Yet what is
refreshing to humans can be devastating to plants.
Seashore winds are laden with salt and rob moisture
from foliage. As a further insult, plants in coastal gardens must cope with hot, sandy soil from which water
and nutrients quickly drain away.

In designing a seashore garden, first examine the
need for a windbreak. If you just want a small,
narrow border along the oceanfront, you will probably not need such protection. After clearing the bed
of its winter accumulation of sand, fill it with sturdy,
low-growing perennials such as Moonbeam coreopsis
and annuals such as portulacas and petunias. (While
these flowers are tough, they are not *that* tough. In the
first year be sure to add good gardening soil to the bed
before planting.)

For more extensive gardens, you will need to build
or plant some sort of protection against both the wind
and the salt air. Tall formal hedges of privet or other
tough evergreens are among the most attractive and
easiest barriers to construct. Step-by-step photos of
hedge planting appear on page 43. Informal
hedgerows of mixed shrubs and shelterbelts with salt-
tolerant trees and shrubs of graduated heights are
other good ways to shield a seaside garden.

*This seashore garden is a riot of color. Plants include catmint
(Nepeta spp.), the tall pink plumes of Filipendula rubra, and
the silvery stems of Russian sage (Perovskia atriplicifolia).*

Seashore Conditions CONTINUED

Plants for Shelter Belts

The following hardy shrubs and small trees will grow by the seaside. When properly planted, they will form a hedge to protect your garden from winds and salt spray.

Serviceberry
(Amelanchier canadensis)
Small tree or shrub with delicate white spring flowers; birds love the red-purple berries.

Cockspur hawthorn
(Crataegus crus-galli)
Native tree that is easily trimmed to serve as a hedge; thorny branches, glossy leaves, and bright red fruit.

Sea buckthorn
(Hippophae rhamnoides)
Spiny shrub with grayish green, willowlike leaves and bright orange berries.

Japanese black pine
(Pinus thunbergiana)
Dense, spreading conifer that thrives near the seashore.

Rugosa rose
(R. rugosa)
Exceptionally hardy and salt-tolerant rose with fragrant flowers in many colors and forms.

In choosing the plants to construct your barrier, decide if you want them to add color to the garden—as rugosa roses do with their flowers, rose hips, and fall foliage—or act as a green backdrop to other plantings, as privet does. Bear in mind that you'll need to trim formal hedges to keep them neat. To avoid trimming, use an informal hedgerow or shelterbelt.

In addition to protecting your garden with a windbreak, you must examine the soil. While quite a few plants can tolerate salt air, only a limited number do well in sand.

If you don't wish to bother with improving your soil, consider creating a container garden. Place large pots about your garden, making sure they are close to a watering mechanism, and then fill them with colorful salt-resistant flowers.

For something a bit grander, you will probably have to work organic matter and clay into your soil to ensure fertility and moisture retention. For low maintenance, keep the borders small and pave the remaining area with white pebbles, brick, or slate.

With the structural elements of your seashore garden in place—a hedge to break the wind, carefully enriched soil in the borders, and attractive paved areas—you can choose the plants to grow. Ask gardening neighbors and friends with oceanfront property about plants that do well while requiring minimal watering and resisting pests and disease. Make a list of these plants, and then consider color, form, and blooming sequence when making your final choices.

A tall hedge makes it possible to grow classic perennials that would not normally thrive in this seaside garden. The hedge shelters the plants from wind and salt.

1 In an exposed location, a hedge of evergreens can protect plants from the damaging effects of wind. Mark off the line of the hedge with stakes and string.

2 Dig a trench instead of individual holes for planting. Loosen the soil in the bottom and sides of the trench. Set a plant in its container in the trench to check depth.

3 Set out the plants alongside the trench and measure to get the correct spacing distance. Allow enough room for plants to grow to their mature size.

4 Remove one plant at a time from its pot, set it in the trench, and fill in around the roots with soil. When all shrubs are planted, firm and rake the soil, and water well.

5 Set up a burlap windscreen on the windward side of the young plants to protect them as they establish new roots and gain a firm foothold in the soil.

6 After several years this arborvitae hedge has grown into an attractive, effective windbreak. Such a hedge can be a wonderful green shield for your other salt-tolerant plants.

Lazy Gardener's Bed

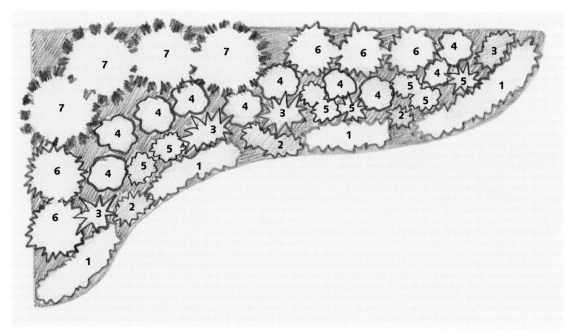

With its profusion of blue and yellow blooms, this garden bed is beautiful both from a distance and up close. When planted along the boundary of a yard, this garden could become an easy-to-maintain privacy screen that will spread and grow.

As winter ebbs, the delicate light blue flowers of glory-of-the-snow will bloom, giving a preview of the burst of flowers to come. Next, the forsythia, with its mass of yellow flowers, heralds the onset of spring. Once the forsythia flowers fade, you'll see a stunning, summer-long display of golden marguerite, accented in early summer by deep purple-blue iris and in mid-summer by the feathery white spires of bottlebrush buckeye. The delicate spikes of Veronica offer a quiet, summer-long complement to the larger, bolder plants in this easy-care garden. The fall-blooming blue spirea closes the show with fragrant violet-blue flowers.

The bottlebrush buckeye is an ideal small, spreading shrub for the backdrop of this easily maintained garden bed. Once this plant is established, it will last for many years without fuss, filling in quite a lot of space if allowed to spread.

Plant List

1 Veronica
(*Veronica spicata*)
2 Glory-of-the-snow
(*Chionodoxa luciliae*)
3 Siberian iris
(*Iris sibirica*)
4 Blue spirea
(*Caryopteris incana*)
5 Golden marguerite
(*Anthemis tinctoria*)
6 Forsythia
(*Forsythia × intermedia*)
7 Bottlebush buckeye
(*Aesculus parviflora*)

The blue spirea needs to be cut back just before winter. It can be pruned right to the ground, which will cause it to bloom even more profusely the following fall. Both its beautiful gray-green leaves and the violet-blue flowers are aromatic. Be careful to avoid soggy conditions as spirea grows best in well-drained soil.

Easy-Care Formal Garden

By combining just a handful of plants in a simple geometric pattern, this easy garden gives the effect of a much more developed and complicated effort. The repetition of plant patterns induces a sense of order and tranquillity to the yard and garden.

The elegant look is reinforced by the choice of only a few subtle colors, as opposed to the profusion of bright colors often found in a cottage garden. In addition, the contrast of textures provides interest even when the blooms are faded. The artemisia forms a soft silver hedge around the beds, contrasting nicely with the white flowers and well-defined bright green leaves of the lily-of-the-valley and the spearlike daylily leaves. This sophisticated garden is easy to start and even easier to maintain.

For best results, follow these simple steps in creating this garden. It's best to plant all the beds in the same year, so that they grow evenly and remain approximately the same size.

1. Put in the path and urn or other focal point, such as a birdbath, sundial, statue, or sculpture.

2. Till the square beds before planting, improving the soil with compost or manure if necessary.

3. First plant the trees in the middle of the beds; add the artemisia next and then the daylilies. Finally, plant the lily-of-the-valley in plugs spaced 6 inches apart.

4. The English ivy surrounding the focal point will last from year to year without trouble. Experiment with different varieties of begonia each year for different colors and different looks.

The path through this garden will be easy to maintain if it's built with a landscape cloth underneath the brick to suppress the weeds. Instead of traditional brick, substitute one of the many available patterns of paving stone or even crushed stone.

The fringe tree is perfect for this garden; because it's slow growing, it won't outgrow the other plants or the scale of the garden. It blooms with showy clusters of fragrant white flowers that hang down below the dark green leaves. In the fall the fringe tree produces dark blue fruits that add another attractive element to the garden.

Plant List
1 Daylily
(Hemerocallis × 'Catherine Woodbury')
2 Silver mound
(Artemisia schmidtiana 'Silver Mound')
3 Fringe tree
(Chionanthus virginicus)
4 Lily-of-the-valley
(Convallaria majalis)
5 Wax begonia
(Begonia × semperflorens-cultorum)
6 English ivy

Weekend-Home Garden

Plant List

1 Sourwood
(Oxydendrum arboreum)
2 Silver lace vine
(Polygonum aubertii)
3 Rugosa rose
(Rosa rugosa)
4 Lilac cranesbill
(Geranium × 'Johnson's Blue')
5 Obedient plant
(Physostegia virginiana)
6 Coralbells
(Heuchera sanguinea)
7 Thyme
(Thymus vulgaris)
8 Threadleaf coreopsis
(Coreopsis verticillata)

Whether you really have a vacation home or just want to feel like you do, here's the perfect garden plan designed for care-free summertime beauty. Not every gardener has the desire or time for spring preparation, summer weeding, or autumn clean-up. This plan is for those who just want to enjoy a trouble-free garden whose beauty will increase year after year.

The plants in this soothing garden have at least three things in common: they are easy to grow, they bloom in the middle of the summer, and they offer old-fashioned appeal. Spending time in this garden is almost like walking into the relaxed, carefree days we remember as children.

The plants in this garden touch and blend with one another, giving a natural, informal atmosphere to the whole summer garden. For example, the thyme invades the lawn somewhat, softening the border between the garden and the grass and eliminates the need for repetitive edging.

As you read a book or sip a lemonade in the filtered shade under the sourwood tree, look up and notice its drooping clusters of white, bell-shaped flowers. The beautiful flowers emit a wonderful fragrance for much of the summer.

A garden like this planted along a fence creates a natural and visually appealing division between the tended landscape and the untended but scenic meadow, field, or farmland beyond.

Kitchen Garden

Why not utilize an area that's often neglected and create a simple kitchen garden by the back door? Here is a mixture of herbs, vegetables, and ornamental (nonedible) flowers that decorates the back entrance and provides a convenient source of fresh-picked table flowers, cooking herbs, or vegetables. Just step outside and grab a sprig of thyme to season a roast, pull up some baby carrots to add to the meal, or pick a fresh bunch of flowers for the centerpiece.

Even a small space can give a lot of pleasure throughout the growing season. After the spears are harvested, the asparagus plant remains a lovely background to this garden, its feathery foliage providing an attractive contrast to the purple-blue salvia flowers and slender, cylindrical leaves of the chives and onions. Try adding some of the asparagus foliage to cut flower arrangements; it adds fullness to the bouquet and looks particularly lovely with the poppies.

A kitchen garden is a wonderful way to introduce a child to gardening, but be sure to instruct the child not to eat or taste anything from the garden without first making sure that it's safe.

Plant List

1 Asparagus
2 Annual candytuft
(Iberis umbellata)
3 Shallots
4 Beets
5 Mealy-cup sage
(Salvia farinacea)
6 Chives
7 Onions
8 Carrots
9 Parsley
10 Leaf lettuce
11 Garlic
12 California poppy
(Eschscholzia californica)
13 Thyme

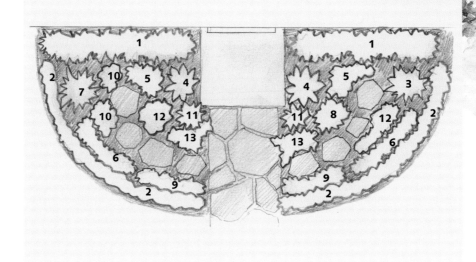

The flowers in this garden are not intended to be edible. There are, however, many varieties of edible flowers available. If you want to alter this plan and substitute edible flowers or other herbs, consult a good book on the subject. Be cautious before consuming any plants to make absolutely certain they are edible.

For a variation in this plan, custom-design a kitchen garden for your own particular tastes. If you like Italian cooking, try growing no-fuss Italian ingredients and flavorings, such as garlic, basil, tomatoes, and onions.

CHAPTER 2

Low-Maintenance Plants

*t*hanks to the existence of thousands of beautiful plants that grow and thrive with little or no pampering from humans, gardening can be manageable for almost anyone. To keep your gardening tasks simple, choose these no-fuss plants. • This chapter gives you guidelines on what kinds of plants to choose and what characteristics to look for to ensure an easy-care garden. As you will see, what is low maintenance in one garden is not necessarily so in another. Be sure you have read Chapter One and considered all the elements of designing your garden before choosing the plants that will go into it. • Throughout this chapter you'll find references to the encyclopedia of plants, which can be found in the back of this book. This chart contains detailed descriptions of superb low-maintenance plants, many of which are perfect candidates for your garden.

Trees and Shrubs

Tree and Shrub Shapes
Here are some suggestions for easy-care trees and shrubs of various basic shapes.

Vase-shaped:
common witch hazel
(Hamamelis virginiana),
Chinese witch hazel
(Hamamelis mollis 'Pallida'),
and Japanese zelkova
(Zelkova serrata).

Weeping:
sargent weeping hemlock
(Tsuga canadensis 'Pendula')
and a crabapple (Malus 'Red
Jade') *developed by the
Brooklyn Botanic Garden in
New York.*

Columnar to pyramidal:
river birch (Betula nigra),
quaking aspen (Populus
tremuloides), *and fringe tree*
(Chionanthus virginicus).

Spreading:
bur oak (Quercus macro-
carpa), *box elder* (Acer
negundo), *mountain maple*
(Acer spicatum), *and serviceberry* (Amelanchier
canadensis).

*T*rees and shrubs are the building blocks of a garden. They are larger than other kinds of plants and are visible in all seasons. They are also expensive, which means that you'll have to give more forethought to purchasing trees and shrubs than any other kinds of plants for your garden.

You may wish to obtain professional help and consult a landscape architect when adding trees and shrubs to your property. However, although trained to give superb advice on placing plants, these experts are not always knowledgeable about which plants you should choose. Too often they settle for what's available at a local nursery and then instruct you to regularly spray, fertilize, and prune. This is not low-maintenance gardening!

To ensure beautiful plantings on your property that require little effort, find out which trees and shrubs grow well in your area. Your local county cooperative extension office (you'll find the number in the county government listings in your phone book), local newspaper columns, regional gardening books, and gardening friends and neighbors are all good sources.

Pay attention to three areas when researching local trees and shrubs: appearance, health, and tidiness.

How the trees and shrubs will actually look in your garden (their appearance) is your first consideration. Trees and shrubs grow in many beautiful and intriguing forms, as shown in the photographs on pages 56–57. As a low-maintenance gardener, you want to make sure that your trees and shrubs attain their forms naturally and not as a result of endless pruning and clipping. Indeed, ban any plant that requires constant shaping from your garden.

Lespedeza thunbergii *has a graceful, fountainy form.*

*Some yews (*Taxus spp.*) have a neat, pyramid shape.*

This specimen of Taxus × media *is broad but strongly upright.*

Because they are so large, the year-round appearance of trees and shrubs is an important consideration. Conifers are superb because they provide a constant green backdrop. One popular evergreen for American gardens is the arborvitae *(Thuja spp.)*. The native arborvitae *(T. occidentalis)* does best in cooler regions, while the Japanese species (usually sold as *T. orientalis* but correctly classified as *Platycladus orientalis*) is better suited for southern states.

To add a bit of flair to your landscape, consider placing an easy-care deciduous tree or shrub near a conifer planting. The beautiful bridal-wreath *(Spirea × vanhouttei)*, for example, is covered with sparkling white flowers in spring. A backing of evergreen conifers not only helps to highlight the spring flowers but also provides a textural contrast throughout the rest of the year.

Selecting trees and shrubs that are healthy is the second consideration when choosing plants. Low-maintenance gardeners can't afford to have sick plants. They take too much time and effort to restore to health and good looks.

One of the easiest ways to determine which trees and shrubs in your area resist pests, have no need for fertilizers, and rarely get sick is to walk through a nearby woods or nature preserve. Plants in such settings have to survive on their own; they're the kind you want in your garden. Take pictures of particularly handsome trees or shrubs and then have a garden center, landscape architect, or cooperative extension office agent identify them.

Juniperus communis 'Compressa' is a dwarf juniper with a narrow columnar form.

Branches of weeping blue atlas cedar (Cedrus atlantica 'Glauca Pendula') droop to the ground.

Shore juniper (Juniperus conferta) is low and spreading, and a good ground cover.

Blue-mist shrub (Caryopteris × clandonensis) is low and bushy.

Trees and Shrubs CONTINUED

Trees and shrubs bring delicate color to a spring landscape. Shown are a pink-flowered azalea (Rhododendron canescens), *white-flowering dogwood* (Cornus florida), *and willow oak* (Quercus phellos) *with its young foliage.*

Also do research to learn which trees and shrubs are native to your area and therefore probably the healthiest and most disease resistant. The serviceberry *(Amelanchier canadensis),* for example, is native to the eastern United States from Maine to Alabama and west to Oklahoma. This large geographic distribution gives some indication of the serviceberry's high resistance to disease and insects, as well as wind and ice.

Once you establish that a tree or shrub is a healthy variety, consider its other attributes. The serviceberry, for example, is great for shaded settings, is covered with white flowers in mid-spring, bears purple berries in summer that attract songbirds, and has colorful orange to dull red foliage in the fall. Consult your local county cooperative extension office, as well as the encyclopedia section of this book (pages 98–126), for information on beautiful, sturdy plants native to your area.

There are also many imported trees and shrubs, particularly from Asia, that may be both beautiful and healthy on your property. Breeders have created superb cultivars that are everything a low-maintenance gardener could ask for.

A good source for recommendations for the best of these imported plants is the Pennsylvania Horticultural Society's Gold Medal Award program. The program honors underutilized trees and shrubs that are hardy, handsome, little known, and perhaps most important, low maintenance.

While it is useful to know that witch hazels *(Hamamelis)* are low-maintenance plants, the Gold Medal Award program goes further and examines specific cultivars. Two that have received recognition are Diane and Pallida. The former *(H. × intermedia* 'Diane') is a 15-foot-tall, vase-shaped hybrid that

The trees shown here are all sturdy, adaptable, and easy to grow. Pictured clockwise from top left are tamarisk or salt cedar (Tamarix), *sugar maple* (Acer saccharum), *white oak* (Quercus alba), *American beech* (Fagus grandifolia), *and Chinese dogwood* (Cornus kousa *var.* chinensis).

Substitutes for Problem Trees

Trees such as white birch, flowering dogwood, and Dutch elm have all been plagued with pests and diseases in recent years. If your property has pest problems, consider planting the following beautiful but tough trees as substitutes.

Heritage river birch (Betula nigra 'Heritage') *Handsome white bark exfoliates and reveals multicolored inner bark.*

Giant dogwood (Cornus controversa) *The branches in this species are layered and bear small white flowers and bright red fall foliage.*

Shademaster honey locust (Gleditsia triacanthos *var.* inermis 'Shademaster') *This thornless, feathery cultivar was bred as an alternative to the Dutch elm.*

bears lots of deep red flowers with ribbonlike petals in late January. The latter *(H. mollis* 'Pallida'*)* flowers in the beginning of February and often holds its pale yellow blooms until mid-March. Both plants are spectacular in barren winter landscapes.

In addition to considering a plant's appearance and health, also take its tidiness into account. When a group of plants exhibits all the neatness of a teenager's bedroom, it can no longer be classified as a low-maintenance garden. To save yourself many hours of cleanup, before you buy a plant consider its extent and kind of leaf fall, the invasiveness of its suckers, and number of self-sown seedlings.

The rose-of-Sharon *(Hibiscus syriacus)*, for example, is a sturdy, attractive shrub. It is covered with lovely large pink or white flowers from summer into fall, does not need to be pruned, and grows without care in a wide variety of light, soil, and moisture conditions. Should you plant such a seemingly low-maintenance performer by a garden path, however, you would soon find a mess of fallen flowers

along the walkway. In damp weather, the flowers become slimy and slippery. This unattractive flower fall is soon followed by fertile seeds. Within a year or two, you will find many—far too many—self-sown rose-of-Sharon seedlings scattered about. Thus, although you'll have little to do to maintain the rose-of-Sharon shrub, you'll spend hours cleaning up after it. As the old saying goes, neatness counts—especially in a low-maintenance garden.

There is a happy ending to the rose-of-Sharon story, however. The U.S. National Arboretum has introduced a rose-of-Sharon cultivar called Diana *(H. syriacus* 'Diana'*)*; it produces large lustrous white flowers that stay open so long they often catch the ethereal light of the summer moon. The flowers are sterile, so you don't have to worry about seedlings. Keep this shrub away from a path and you'll have a magnificent border specimen.

Perennials

TROUBLESHOOTING TIP

When adding new perennials to your garden, look for those designated as Perennial Plant of the Year selections. These are flowers honored by the Perennial Plant Association for their beauty, their long season of interest, and their low-maintenance requirements. The selections are widely available at garden centers and through mail-order nurseries. Past winners have included Moonbeam coreopsis and Palace Purple heuchera.

*H*undreds of varieties of perennials require little or no maintenance. For an easy-care garden, choose only those perennials that bloom for a long period of time, are widely adaptable, require little or no deadheading, and rarely need to be staked or divided. The plant encyclopedia on pages 98–126 describes in more detail nearly 50 of these lovely fuss-free perennial flowers.

As with other plants, however, low-maintenance perennials need to be given a proper home to do their best. The care-free wild bleeding-heart *(Dicentra eximia)*, for example, requires humusy soil and heavy doses of shade to produce its exquisite blooms, which resemble pink teardrops and last for eight or more weeks in spring.

Moonbeam coreopsis, on the other hand, needs full sun and well-drained soil to encourage the arrival of its pale yellow daisy flowers, which last from summer through early frosts. Put the coreopsis next to a bleeding-heart in a woodland garden and it will do nothing for you.

Other low-maintenance perennials, such as the Lancaster geranium *(G. sanguineum* var. *striatum)*, also grow beautifully under proper conditions, but perform less spectacularly when planted in a less hospitable setting. In full sun, the Lancaster geranium sends out its soft pink flowers from late spring well into fall. Give this plant a lot of shade, however, and its bloom period will be significantly shortened. In either condition the geranium will require little work on your part; but when it is deprived of sun, you may have to add other plants, such as shade-tolerant impatiens, to keep the garden colorful all season.

Daylilies (Hemerocallis *spp.) are among the easiest perennials to grow. They bloom beautifully in either full sun or partial shade, adapt to a wide range of soil types, and can be left alone for years before they need division.*

1 *Some nonhybrid perennials, like purple coneflower (Echinacea purpurea), will self-sow if you don't deadhead them (a great excuse to save yourself some work).*

2 *When the volunteer seedlings are a few inches high, dig them up in clumps, and replace any soil disturbed around the parent plant.*

3 *Tease apart the seedlings, working gently to minimize damage to roots.*

4 *Transplant the seedlings to a suitable location, and you will be rewarded with a free crop of flowers next year.*

TIMESAVING TIP

Use mulch to control the number of self-sown seedlings from your favorite perennials. If you find you have too many self-seeders, mulch heavily when the seedlings are still tiny. If you want more plants, don't mulch at all so that seeds can sprout on the bare earth.

Perennials CONTINUED

Calla lilies (Zantedeschia) *and a white-flowered variety of veronica* (Veronica) *thrive in the moist soil and open, sunny conditions of this garden.*

Foxgloves (Digitalis *spp.*) *are biennials, but they self-sow freely and come back year after year as if they were perennials.*

Catmints (Nepeta *spp.*) *bloom long and profusely in summer. To eliminate the work of deadheading, cut back the plants after the first flush of bloom and they will flower again with renewed vigor.*

Annuals

Exercise care when fertilizing annuals. Too much nitrogen generally causes lots of lush foliage growth and little flower development. Use a fertilizer with a higher concentration of phosphorus, which helps flowering. Or work colloidal or rock phosphate into the soil the autumn before planting.

*A*n annual is a plant that completes its life cycle in a single year. An annual germinates, sets flowers, produces seed, then dies at the end of the growing season (although many gardeners also count biennials and perennials that will bloom the first year from seed as annuals). Because an annual's mission is to produce seeds, it will continue to bloom if faded flowers are clipped off before seeds mature. That's why so many annuals bloom all summer long, some even without deadheading. Although annuals must be planted each year, they flower lavishly all summer long, and most are very easy to care for.

Left to their own devices, many annual flowers could not survive in northern climates. There simply is not enough time for them to complete their necessary growing cycles. The development of the greenhouse in the early nineteenth century made it possible to extend the growing season by germinating annuals in a protected environment indoors and then setting them out in the garden when warm spring temperatures arrived.

Low-maintenance gardeners recognize that annuals are truly the colorful workhorses in gardens. Don't feel bound by old-fashioned conventions that dictate a flower bed must be all annuals or all perennials. If you want easy-care color, a mixed border, in which annuals, perennials, and bulbs beautifully coexist, is probably perfect for you.

The development of sterile cultivars has made it even easier to include annuals in mixed flower gardens without making more work. Sterile annual cultivars cannot produce seed, but the plants keep producing flowers in the vain hope that they will finally be able

Salvia farinacea 'Victoria', grown as an annual in the North, flowers all summer until frost. The long-lasting flowers eliminate the need for frequent deadheading.

Annuals CONTINUED

to set seed. Though they never reach their goal, the gardener is rewarded with a continued succession of blossoms without any ugly seed heads or unwanted self-sown seedlings.

Much work in the development of easy-care attributes in annual plants has been carried out under the auspices of the All-America Selections program. Started in 1933 and located in Downers Grove, Illinois, this organization sponsors a network of test gardens across North America where new flower and vegetable cultivars are grown before they enter commercial production. The varieties producing the best results are declared All-America Selections winners. AAS winners have proven superior qualities, including beauty, adaptability to many climate conditions, and resistance to pests and diseases. They are generally good bets for low-maintenance gardens.

Recent AAS annual flower winners include Lady in Red salvia *(S. coccinea* 'Lady in Red'*)*, whose spikes of bright red flowers attract both butterflies and hummingbirds, and Castle Pink celosia *(C.* 'Castle Pink'*)*, a heat- and drought-tolerant plant with a 7-inch central plume that can be cut for fresh or dried flowers. These are both superb plants for low-maintenance gardens because they do not need to be deadheaded or staked.

Decorative Annual Foliage

Don't overlook the decorative qualities of colored and variegated foliage when choosing annuals for the garden. Plants grown primarily for their foliage are attractive all season and generally need little maintenance. Possibilities include green and white snow-on-the-mountain (Euphorbia marginata); *purple-leaved perilla* (Perilla frutescens); *tricolor sage* (Salvia officinalis 'Tricolor'), *with cream, purple, and green leaves;*

deep burgundy beefsteak plant (Iresine herbstii); *and the many gorgeous patterned cultivars of coleus* (C. × hybridus), *some of which are shown at left.*

In addition, some annuals grown for their flowers also contribute ornamental foliage to the garden. Some cultivars of wax begonia (Begonia × semperflorens-cultorum) *have deep, lustrous bronze leaves. Zonal geraniums* (Pelargonium × hortorum) *are*

common bedding geraniums that have dark bands on their leaves. Another fancy-leaved annual is any cultivar of New Guinea hybrid impatiens, a sun-tolerant impatiens with leaves striped in gold or red.

Many annuals, including those shown here, bloom all summer. This garden contains petunias, marigolds, wax begonias, ageratum, impatiens, and geraniums.

TIMESAVING TIP

For the widest selection of annuals, grow your own from seeds started early indoors or sown directly in the garden. If you want to plant coleus in a shady spot, for example, you will probably find that seed catalogues carry many more different kinds than your local garden center. You can experiment with different types every year, or take cuttings in early fall of a variety you especially like. Root the cuttings in water, pot up the plants to use indoors in winter, and move them out to the garden next spring.

Of course, what grows as an annual in some parts of the country may last longer in other places. Flowers such as red ginger *(Alpinia purpurata)* and Peruvian lily *(Alstroemeria psittacina)* are perennials in Florida and southern California but must be treated as annuals in cooler climates farther north. Others, such as Victoria salvia *(S. farinacea* 'Victoria'*)*, are middle-of-the-road plants; that is, sometimes they survive winters as far north as New Jersey and sometimes they don't.

If there's some question about the hardiness of a plant that you're planning to include in your design scheme, classify it as an annual. That way, you won't be disappointed if it doesn't come back and will have already planned on replacing it each year.

A truly exceptional plant for any flower garden—perennial or annual—is the Victoria salvia. This plant exhibits all the no-fuss qualities you should be looking for when choosing annuals for your low-maintenance garden. It is exceptionally easy to grow—you can just plant it and forget it. Should drought conditions occur in your area, you would probably have to water this plant once a week. Its 1½-foot stems are sturdy and rarely require staking. While there is absolutely no need to deadhead the plant, you may well want to cut some of its attractive spikes of blue flowers—which appear from late spring through light frosts—for indoor arrangements.

As with perennials, trees, and shrubs, select annuals that are disease resistant to minimize the amount of tending your garden will need. For example, the self-reliant Victoria salvia, with its attractive blue-green foliage, is rarely bothered by pests or diseases and is therefore appropriate for a no-fuss garden.

Bulbs

*B*ulbs are wonderful stalwarts in low-maintenance gardens. Hardy bulbs come back year after year with very little work on your part, and the plantings even increase in size over the years. Once in a while you will need to divide clumps of bulbs that become crowded, but division will give you more bulbs to plant in other parts of the garden. For care-free color, bulbs are one of the best investments you can make.

In cooler climates hardy bulbs are one of the easiest plants to grow. Spring bloomers include crocuses, snowdrops, narcissus and daffodils, tulips, and hyacinths. Summer brings magnificent lilies. There are also some delightful autumn-flowering bulbs, such as autumn crocuses *(Crocus spp.)* and colchicums *(Colchicum spp.)*, which are similar to crocuses but have larger flowers.

Gardeners who live where winters are warm can fill beds with tender bulbs such as summer caladiums, gladiolus, tuberous begonias, and cannas, and leave the bulbs in the ground all year. In cooler climates these tender bulbs must be dug up and stored indoors over winter, and replanted in spring. Although certain varieties of daffodils and lilies flourish in warm climates, some hardy bulbs that are easy to grow in the North take more work. Tulips and hyacinths, for example, must be refrigerated before planting to give them the necessary cold period that will enable them to bloom, and they are unlikely to come back a second year in a warm-climate garden.

1 *One daffodil bulb will eventually grow into a clump of flowers. When bloom declines, dig up an old, crowded planting and divide the bulbs.*

2 *Prepare the soil in the expanded planting area, and for a natural look, scatter the divided bulbs by handfuls over the ground.*

3 *Plant the bulbs where they fall. As the years go by, the daffodils will naturalize to create a river of brilliant yellow blossoms each spring.*

If you choose bulbs suited to your climate, though, you can bring explosions of seasonal color to your garden with minimal maintenance. You will become part of a proud American gardening tradition.

Bulbs have been important plants in American gardens since colonial days. Thomas Jefferson relied on bulbs to beautify the grounds at Monticello, his estate near Charlottesville, Virginia. With bulbs he was assured of persistent low-maintenance color.

Although Jefferson favored large swaths of tulips, most low-maintenance gardeners today cannot indulge in such luxury. Too frequently, these gorgeous bulbs are eaten by deer and other animal pests. Unless you wish to fence in your property and plant your bulbs in wire-mesh cages, avoid these pretty flowers where animal predators abound.

Fortunately, hundreds of other colorful bulbs are perfect for easy-care gardens. Daffodils, for example, are poisonous to most animal pests. In addition, there is a wide range of daffodil species whose flowers come back each spring year after year (many tulips, on the other hand, have to be replanted annually). These species also "naturalize" readily, reproducing and spreading on their own, as they do in the wild.

Wood hyacinths *(Endymion hispanicus)*, another care-free bulb, follow daffodils in the seasonal blooming parade. Close cousins to English bluebells *(E. nonscriptus)*, wood hyacinths produce white, blue, or pink flowers in sun or shade and are rarely bothered by pests or diseases.

Flowering onions *(Allium* spp.*)* are another group of garden gems that deer, rodents, and other animals avoid. There are more than 300 different kinds of alliums, bearing flowers in a rainbow of colors—blues, violets, reds, pinks, yellows, and whites. Bloom time for these plants varies from spring through fall.

Narcissus *'Barrett Browning'* sports a bright orange corona ("cup") and naturalizes readily.

N. *'Jenny', another good naturalizer, blends a creamy perianth ("petals") with a soft yellow cup.*

N. *'Thalia' is creamy white, fragrant, and also good for naturalizing.*

And although some emit an onion fragrance when cut, others, such as daffodil garlic *(A. neapolitanum)*, are sweetly fragrant. Daffodil garlic has sprays of white starlike flowers that open in May and are often used in bridal bouquets in Europe.

Colchicums, often incorrectly called fall crocuses, are perfect bulbs for the end of the garden year. They are poisonous to animals (people, too) and therefore are rodent-proof. Colchicums bear large, lustrous chalice-shaped flowers in September and October and are charming when they pop up amid green ground covers such as pachysandra. *Colchicum* 'Waterlily' is especially lovely—its pointed petals open wide like the petals of its namesake.

The plant encyclopedia section beginning on page 98 describes in detail many bulbs that would be excellent candidates for a low-maintenance garden.

Ornamental Grasses

*A*merican gardeners can thank German nurseryman Karl Foerster for transforming our idea of grasses from a flat expanse of uniform green lawn to towering fountains of many-colored and textured leaves. In the 1920s, when most Americans were unaware of the beauty of waving plumes of tall field grasses, European gardeners—guided by Foerster—were creating exquisite grass gardens.

A half-century later, American gardeners began to combine these easy-care grasses with low-maintenance perennials in dynamic gardens that seem perfectly suited to today's busy, informal lifestyles. The "new American garden," as it is called, features drifts of low-maintenance plants in combinations designed to be of interest all year.

From summer through much of winter, ornamental grasses are standouts in low-maintenance gardens. The grasses need virtually no care, except to be cut back to the ground in early spring. In addition to their graceful forms and soothing colors, the grasses bring movement and sound to the garden when the wind blows. Tall-growing grasses offer privacy as well. One delightful species, feather reed grass *(Calamagrostis acutiflora)*, starts to bear fluffy bluish flower panicles in June; these age to a lovely golden tan. The dried stand of grass looks handsome in the garden all winter. There are several sterile cultivars of this very easy-to-grow plant. One, which reaches 6 feet tall, is appropriately named 'Karl Foerster.'

Once ornamental grasses become established there should be little need for weeding. Before planting grasses, however, clear the area of any weeds. You may need to pull stray weeds while the grasses are young, but if planted close enough together, the grasses will block germination of weed seeds when they reach mature size.

In the encyclopedia section (pages 98-126), you'll find descriptions of several ornamental grasses that provide color and texture, can naturalize on slopes, are perfect for seashore gardens, or are at home in shade or boggy conditions. Be sure, however, the ornamental grasses you choose are suited to your growing conditions.

Ornamental grasses need little upkeep, and the tall ones afford privacy as well.

Instead of a labor-intensive expanse of lawn, consider planting ornamental grasses in a low-traffic area. Grasses provide many different textures and subtle colors.

Herbs

*H*erbs are usually described as plants that are grown for culinary, medicinal, or craft uses. They are, in other words, practical as well as beautiful. They are also, for the most part, low maintenance. The volatile oils in their leaves and stems, which give them their characteristic scents, flavors, and healing properties, in many cases repel insects, too. And herbs are seldom threatened by disease.

Given their multiplicity of uses, herbs fit well in an ornamental bed or border or a vegetable garden. But wherever you plant your herbs, give them full sun and soil with excellent drainage. (Some herbs, such as mint, will also grow in shade. See the plant encyclopedia beginning on page 98 for more information on chives, sweet woodruff, garlic, parsley, and thyme.)

The kind of garden in which you grow herbs will determine the size of the planting. If you are growing herbs solely for culinary purposes, you should plant only the quantity you need to feed your family. On the other hand, if you wish to incorporate herbs into an ornamental border, you can easily have sizable drifts of them floating through the garden. Thus, while you might only need two or three curly-leaf

parsley plants in a low-maintenance vegetable garden, where space is at a premium, you could easily plant a winding stream of their rich green leaves to wander about a sunny grouping of colorful annuals.

Whether its purpose is utilitarian or ornamental, the appropriateness of a particular herb for low-maintenance gardens depends upon two key points: will it spread and will it self-seed?

While seed or plant catalogues may hesitate to use the word "invasive," phrases such as "spreads rapidly" should warn you that a particular herb is not suitable for a low-maintenance garden. All varieties of mints *(Mentha* spp.*),* for example, are notorious wanderers. Easy to care for in every other aspect, they can take over a garden if not properly confined. Yet these herbs are perfect candidates for pots and containers.

With self-seeders, consider how easy it will be to remove seedlings that pop up where you don't want them, and whether you think the plant looks attractive in your garden. Dill *(Anethum graveolens),* for example, has a long taproot that is easy to pull up and doesn't interfere with the roots of other nearby plants; its delicate, lacy blue-green foliage is attractive both in

The four herbs shown here need little maintenance when planted in a congenial site. Left to right: thyme, chives, parsley, and oregano.

Herbs combine readily with flowers in a relaxed, informal bed. Feathery fennel leaves, left, add height and texture, and chives contribute their vertical line with purple flowers in early summer.

informal settings and in flower arrangements. While you certainly would not want dill sprouting up everywhere in a formal herb garden, it can be an attractive seasoning source in a more relaxed planting.

Garlic chives *(Allium tuberosum)* produce lovely starry white flowers in late summer. Let them go to seed, however, and the straplike foliage will pop up everywhere. A member of the onion family, this plant is not easily pulled out. If you don't remove the bulb underground, new leaves will grow. Ordinary chives *(A. schoenoprasum)* self-sow less readily. These easy-to-grow herbs have round heads of purple-pink flowers in early summer.

Of course, you can keep all these self-seeding plants from spreading simply by cutting off the flower heads. But if this sounds like too much of a chore, leave the self-sowers out of your garden.

Vegetables

Green Manure

A very effective soil enrichment technique is to plant grasses, called "green manure," as a cover crop during the winter months. Till your cleared garden beds after fall harvest and thickly broadcast, or scatter, grass seeds. Turn the young green shoots under in early spring, or cut them back to the ground a month or so before planting your garden. The shoots will quickly break down and enrich your soil. Popular cover crops include annual rye, hairy vetch, winter barley, buckwheat, clover, and alfalfa. Call your county cooperative extension agent to see what grass is best for your area.

Growing your own vegetables opens up all sorts of culinary possibilities. Homegrown vegetables taste better than the ones in the supermarket (think about tomatoes!) and can be more nutritious too. Growing your own vegetables also gives you much greater variety than you would find in a supermarket. For a low-maintenance garden, however, you want to grow vegetables that are easy to care for.

Old-fashioned varieties are among the easiest to maintain. These are vegetables that were grown a century or more ago, before finicky hybrids were so omnipresent. In those days, vegetables that thrived did so without the use of fertilizers or pesticides; they were simply naturally strong and resistant. Some newer varieties are bred for disease and pest resistance, but many still have problems.

Seed for many heirloom vegetables is available from the Seed Savers Exchange. This nonprofit organization is a clearinghouse for members seeking to offer and obtain seed. The annual catalogue of available seeds often exceeds 250 pages of single-spaced listings (see page 128 for more information).

Another way to find reliable varieties when buying plants at a garden center or ordering seeds through the mail is to look for All-America Selections winners, indicated by a logo with the letters "AAS." As explained on page 64, a plant so honored has been tested throughout the United States and judged to be superior in quality and easy to grow.

Always check for phrases such as "disease resistant" in a vegetable plant's description. With tomatoes, look for the initials "VFNT," which mean that

Peas are undemanding in the garden, and their flowers are quite pretty. If planted in fertile soil next to a trellis, they need little except for watering during dry spells.

Purple vegetables are not only decorative but also reputedly less troubled by pests and diseases than their conventionally colored counterparts. Shown here, clockwise from top left, are purple cauliflower, a burgundy-tipped leaf lettuce, red-veined cabbage, and purple-podded snap beans.

the plant is resistant to two wilt diseases (*Verticillium* and *Fusarium*), an insect (nematodes), and a plant virus (tobacco mosaic virus).

When possible, avoid vegetable plants that need to be staked or supported. Breeders have developed bush varieties of beans, peas, and even squashes. The bush forms may not be as prolific as the vining kinds, but they require much less maintenance.

Another work saver is to choose vegetables that do not need daily harvesting. Bush forms of Italian-type beans, often called romano or roma beans, produce delicious pods that can be harvested early or allowed to remain on their stems for a week longer with no loss of quality. Regular snap beans, on the other hand, need to be picked almost daily or they quickly become tough and seedy.

Peppers are another vegetable that can withstand a neglectful harvester. If picked at an immature stage, the green fruits are hard and crisp—and very refreshing on hot summer days. If allowed to ripen over several weeks, peppers become wonderfully sweet and turn brilliant red, yellow, purple, or orange.

When selecting a low-maintenance variety of tomato, avoid "determinate" tomatoes. These plants bear all their fruit at once and then stop producing; you'll pick furiously for a week and then have nothing afterward. Look for tomato plants that are described as "indeterminate"; the plants take longer to grow, but they keep producing until the cold weather arrives.

Finally, choose vegetables that are suitable to the season. Lettuces, peas, and radishes, for example, like to grow in cool weather. No matter how prolific or pest- and disease-resistant individual varieties are, they will all struggle in hot, humid summer weather. Black-seeded Simpson lettuce *(Lactuca sativa)*, for example, has been a staple in American spring vegetable gardens for more than 100 years; as soon as hot weather strikes, however, it produces seed and is useless as a vegetable. Similarly, tomatoes, melons, and peppers are warm-weather plants. If you tempt fate and plant these vegetables outdoors in a cool spring, you are only inviting disaster.

Include perennial vegetables in your garden if you have room. Two long-lived vegetables that are relatively free of maintenance are asparagus and rhubarb. When planting asparagus, choose the disease-resistant Mary Washington cultivar.

CHAPTER 3

Techniques That Lower Maintenance

gardening should be a pleasure rather than a chore; this chapter will show you timesaving tips that will make gardening enjoyable. Commonsense time- and labor-saving techniques are used by all savvy gardeners, even those who have extravagantly lush gardens with finicky plants. • The goal of low-maintenance gardening is to work *with* nature, not against it. Because most plants do best in reasonably fertile, well-drained soil, it only makes sense to create an ideal setting before planting flowers or vegetables. • Use the information, tips, and techniques in this chapter to create your own beautiful and productive garden, one that will bring you great joy rather than frustration.

Soil

*I*f you properly prepare your garden soil before you start to plant, you'll save yourself endless hours and considerable expense in trying to make up for deficiencies later.

Of course, there are plants for just about every soil condition, and you can simply choose plants to fit the ground in which you are working. However, you may find that the range of available plants suited to your existing soil conditions is exceedingly limited. There's a lot you can do to improve the overall quality of your soil, and starting with good soil will greatly broaden your plant choices.

To find out the type of soil in your garden, and determine whether you need to improve it before planting, conduct four basic soil tests.

Start by seeing how well the soil drains after a heavy rainstorm (or after you have doused it with water from a hose or bucket). If the water seeps down at a steady rate, your soil has good drainage, and it may be sandy. Sandy soil provides lots of room for roots to move about, but it tends to contain few nutrients for plants because in the porous structure they wash away with the draining water.

If the soil holds puddles for a long time, it's probably heavy and contains clay. Clay soil is loaded with nutrients, but its dense structure can be so unyielding that roots barely penetrate it. If your soil is either very sandy or heavy with clay, improvements are in order to make the soil hospitable to garden plants.

For the second test, turn over some soil with a spade or trowel and see if you can find earthworms in it. These wonderful creatures are a necessity in a low-maintenance garden. Their digestive enzymes chemically alter soil components in a plant's favor, and their burrowing activities significantly improve soil drainage and aeration. Consider yourself lucky if your

soil already contains lots of earthworms; if not, you'll want to improve your soil to attract them.

Next test aspects of your soil's fertility. You can buy a soil-testing kit from a local garden center or hardware store, but be sure to buy a good one. The very cheap ones are less informative and less reliable. An alternative is to have your soil tested by your local county cooperative extension. You can also have the soil tested by a private laboratory.

Home test kits allow you to test your soil for two factors: pH and key nutrients. The pH scale describes the degree of acidity or alkalinity of the soil. An extremely high (alkaline) or low (acid) pH affects the ability of a plant to absorb essential mineral nutrients from the soil.

The majority of plants grown in North America flourish in soils with a pH ranging between 6 and 7, which is mildly acid to neutral. You can make modest adjustments in pH, but not major alterations. If you live in the Southwest and your soil is strongly alkaline, you won't be able to lower the pH enough to grow azaleas, which thrive in acidic soil. But you can bring your highly alkaline soil closer to neutral. To raise the pH of acid soil, add ground limestone from a local garden center or hardware store, or wood ashes from a fireplace or stove (this is called "sweetening the soil"). To lower the pH of alkaline soil, use powdered sulfur, acid peat moss, or an acid fertilizer. Or mulch your garden with acid-laden pine needles or oak leaves, which will lower the pH as they decompose.

The three major nutrients your plants need are nitrogen, phosphorus, and potassium. Nitrogen is important for leaf and stem growth, phosphorus plays a key role in root development and seed formation (and is thus important for flowering), and potassium enhances plant vigor and resistance to disease. On a

1 Build a compost pile from alternating layers of "wet" material (green plant matter, fruit and vegetable peels, coffee grounds) and dry plant debris.

2 Sprinkle wet layers with wood ashes (for potassium and to lower pH) or lime (to raise pH) and livestock manure, or blood meal (a slaughterhouse by-product), or garden soil.

3 Spray the compost pile with water until it is as moist as a squeezed-out sponge. Moisten the pile whenever it gets dried out.

4 Turn the compost once a week, moving material from the outer edges of the pile into the center. The compost is ready to use once it is dark brown and crumbly.

E A R T H • W I S E
T I P

Organic matter should be continually added to your garden soil. One simple schedule is to add topdressings of composted leaves in the spring, grass clippings in the summer, and dried manure in the fall. Or work compost into the soil in spring and fall, and top-dress in summer when the garden is full of plants.

Soil CONTINUED

bag of fertilizer, the ratio of these nutrients is always expressed in this order—nitrogen (N), phosphorus (P), potassium (K). Thus, 10-10-10 fertilizer has 10 percent of each nutrient mixed with inert filler, and 5-10-5 fertilizer is higher in phosphorus.

The best way to build better soil is to work in lots of organic matter. Organic matter helps solve all sorts of soil problems, such as poor drainage, lack of earthworms, extreme pH levels, or low nutrients. The best source of organic material is a compost pile, which allows you to recycle leaves, grass clippings, plant debris, and household food waste into a nutrient-rich soil conditioner. Follow the step-by-step photos on page 77 to learn how to make a compost pile. Adding compost to your soil every year will keep it in good shape for growing plants.

When soil problems have been corrected and the weather is suitable, you can begin planting. If you are planting trees and shrubs, note that experts now advise against improving the soil *only* in the planting hole. When the roots of large plants go beyond their initial planting spot, which they invariably do, they experience a shock when moving into unamended soil. This shock is detrimental to their growth, and the roots may confine themselves to the initial planting area. If you don't amend the soil in the entire area that could eventually be covered by roots, it's better to place large plants in the same kind of soil that exists in other parts of the garden.

If you're an impatient gardener, you may not want to wait until a compost pile decomposes into rich, crumbly humus and then spend time working the

A seaside location calls for plants that thrive in sandy soil and windy conditions. Ornamental grasses and a shrub rose, 'The Fairy,' are an easy-care combination.

The moisture-holding clay soil of this garden supports lush growth of perennials and ornamental grasses. The addition of organic matter lightens and aerates clay soils.

organic matter into a proposed garden area. Don't despair—there is a low-maintenance alternative. Simply have a load of good-quality topsoil delivered to your property and placed in a raised bed.

Once the garden is established, keep the soil in good shape. Adding compost once a year is the best way to condition the soil, but you can also use an organic mulch during the growing season and leave it in place to decompose. Mulch adds vital nutrients to the soil, smothers weeds, and conserves moisture as plants grow. Mulching can be viewed as a form of slow composting without your having to first place the plant material in a special bin.

Readily available mulches include grass clippings and shredded leaves (many municipalities now make composted leaves available to residents at no charge). Simply collect this material and place it loosely around your plants. Over time, those hardworking little earthworms will work the mulch into your garden soil. If you use grass clippings, spread them in thin layers until they dry out, or they will compact into a slimy dense mat. If you mulch with sawdust, wood chips, or shredded bark, add a nitrogen fertilizer as well, because wood products use up nitrogen from the soil as they decompose.

Planting

Once you've properly prepared the soil, you're ready to begin planting your chosen flowers or vegetables. The basic steps are: digging holes, placing the plants into the ground, firming the soil around the roots, and then watering thoroughly.

Before you place any plant into the ground, make sure that its roots have adequate space and are not tightly packed into their new home. For plants that have been growing in pots, carefully check to see if the roots are loose. If the soil and roots form a compact mass when you remove the plant from its container, gently tease apart some of the roots so that they can spread out. If this treatment doesn't work, you may have to cut some of the root growth away. A root-bound plant, whether a shrub in a large pot or a vegetable in a six-pack container, will most likely die if the roots are not untangled before being put into the ground.

These procedures will make your initial planting successful; the following suggestions should greatly reduce the amount of work needed later.

Clear all weeds from the planting area before putting plants in the ground. It's often difficult to get rid of pernicious pests when they are growing among the roots of valued plants.

A lovely combination of herbs, vegetables, and flowers blends together in a delightfully informal bed. From front to back are lady's-mantle (Alchemilla), *chives, garlic, yarrow* (Achillea), *forget-me-nots* (Myosotis), *and rhubarb in the back with columbines* (Aquilegia) *to the left.*

1 *Intensive planting is an efficient use of garden space. Instead of planting in rows, set plants equidistant from one another in all directions.*

2 *When the plants mature, the close spacing creates a sort of living mulch. The leafy canopy shades the roots to keep them cool and also cuts down on weed growth.*

It is important to time plantings correctly. Tender annuals, bulbs, and vegetables will be damaged or killed by late frost if you plant them too early. A very dependable guide to help you determine when it's safe to plant warm-weather crops is to observe oak trees in your neighborhood. When the oak leaves are as big as a squirrel's ear, that is, an inch or two long, go ahead and plant. Oak trees are the last trees to send out their new leaves in spring; when they do, the danger of frost is almost certainly past.

Avoid planting large areas with just one kind of flower or vegetable. If a disease or animal predator strikes a particular type of plant, the whole planting can be quickly wiped out. Gardens that mix different plants are a safer bet.

From a low-maintenance standpoint it's best to choose young plants for your garden. It's harder for a mature specimen, with its extensive root system, to settle into a new home. Seedlings or young plants suffer less transplant shock and adapt more quickly to new surroundings.

Most gardens have two kinds of plants: temporary ones (annual vegetables and flowers) and permanent ones (perennial flowers and trees and shrubs). These two groups require different low-maintenance planting techniques. Here are some tips to help you minimize the attention each type of plant will need.

▼ Temporary Plants

Use the following low-maintenance techniques when planting annual vegetables and flowers.

▼ Rotate your plantings. This technique is particularly appropriate in a vegetable garden, where some plants (called heavy feeders) take a lot of nutrients from the soil as they grow, some (light feeders) take fewer nutrients, and others (members of the legume family) actually return nutrients in the soil. Planting several heavy feeders in succession can deplete the soil's nutrient supply. Instead, plant beans, peas, or a cover crop like alfalfa to increase the soil's nitrogen content. You could plant corn in an area one year, then beans and peas the next. The former depletes nitrogen in the soil while the latter add it. Consult a good book on vegetable gardening for specific crop rotation patterns.

Planting CONTINUED

**TROUBLESHOOTING
TIP**

*When planting a ball-and-
burlapped tree, cut and
loosen the burlap and twine,
but don't remove them
entirely. Both the burlap and
the twine will eventually
decompose in the ground.
Make sure the burlap is completely underground; if any
of it protrudes aboveground
it will draw moisture out of
the soil. Cut away the
exposed part of the burlap
and cover firmly with soil.*

Crop rotation also decreases the chances of plant-specific diseases settling into the soil. You might place closely related tomatoes and peppers in one area one year and then the entirely different cole or cabbage family crops (broccoli, kale, cabbage) the next. You might then follow the cole crops with beet or onion family members, or with beans or peas.

▼ Time your plantings to avoid insect invasions. Leaf miners, for example, destroy spinach leaves. But these pests don't appear until warm weather has fully settled in. Because spinach prefers cool weather, plant it in early spring and again in fall. Once warm weather comes, pull out the remaining plants to destroy any potential homes for the leaf miner.

▼ Practice intensive and succession planting. The goal of intensive planting is to use space efficiently. Instead of planting wide-spaced single rows of vegetables, plant bands or blocks where the plants are equidistant. The photos on page 81 show how to do intensive planting. Succession planting is simply following one crop with another. When you pull out that early spinach, for example, put in tomatoes or eggplants, which thrive in warm weather. Using intensive and succession planting reduces the size of the growing area you must maintain, and the closeness of the plants gives weeds less room to grow.

▼ **Permanent Plants**
The following tips apply to perennial flowers and trees and shrubs—plants that will remain in place for at least three or four years.

▼ If you are creating a mixed bed or border, plant trees and shrubs first, as they require the largest area of preparation. By starting off with them, you won't need to disturb the roots of other plants.

▼ Layer your plantings to have continuous color in a smaller space. Place shallow-rooted, early-blooming plants above deeper-rooted bulbs or perennials that emerge later. For example, crocuses, winter aconites (*Eranthis hyemalis*), and Virginia bluebells (*Mertensia virginica*) can be planted above lilies and hostas. Bedding annuals can be planted over narcissus and tulips. By layering you can concentrate plants that appear in different seasons in one area, instead of scattering them around the property. Be careful not to disturb the deeper roots when planting over them.

Place plants at the correct depth, so that they grow properly and flower longer. This is particularly important for peonies and bulbs. If you plant a peony too deeply, it will have lush foliage but no flowers. If you plant bulbs too shallowly, they will bloom for only one season at most. You can continue the blooming life of many tulips for many years by planting them 8 inches deep.

1 When planting a young tree, dig a hole a bit deeper than the rootball and twice as wide. Loosen the soil around the sides of the hole to encourage roots to grow.

2 Mix the soil excavated from the hole with organic matter, including compost or leaf mold, to improve aeration, drainage, and moisture retention.

3 Gently slide the plant out of its container and set it in the planting hole. The plant should sit at the same depth at which it was growing in the nursery.

4 Center the plant in the hole and fill in around the roots with soil. When the hole is halfway filled, fill it to the top with water. When the water drains away, finish filling with soil.

5 Firm the soil around the rootball, by pressing with your feet, to remove air pockets. Trees taller than the one shown should be staked for their first year in the garden.

6 If deer are a problem in your area, surround the newly planted tree with a cylinder of hardware cloth or wire fencing to keep the visitors from nibbling on your plant.

Watering

**TIMESAVING
TIP**

*Healthy lawns survive with
infrequent intervals of heavy
watering. On average, lawns
need about 1 inch of water
per week, either from rainfall
or in combination with other
watering methods.*

Water is essential to the life of your garden, but the
amount required by different plants varies dramatically. Unless your growing area is constantly moist,
it's best to choose plants that don't require frequent
watering. If, however, you can't resist a group of very
thirsty plants, place them together in a specially prepared area that is close to a water source.

A garden composed of good soil and hardy plants
normally requires an average of about 1 inch of water
a week. In the absence of rain, you will have to supply
that water—but only about once a week. When you
do water, however, make sure you water deeply to
supply the equivalent of 1 inch of steady rain that
soaks thoroughly into the soil.

While rain splatters an entire plant, you should not.
The water should be aimed at the ground rather than
at leaf level. Water droplets lingering on foliage, especially at night, are often an open invitation for bac-
teria and viral diseases to settle in and start growing. If
you do use an overhead sprinkler, water at least a few
hours before nightfall, so that the leaves will dry
before dark.

To reduce the necessity of even a weekly watering,
heavily mulch your garden. Mulch provides a protective blanket that slows the evaporation of moisture
from the soil. In addition to using organic mulches
such as compost, shredded leaves, and dried grass clippings, you can use plant foliage to shade and cool the
soil. Hostas, for example, have large leaves that cover
the surrounding ground and act as mulches in their
own right.

If your plants are still thirsty despite being grown in
good soil and protected by mulch, consider installing a
drip-irrigation system. Drip-irrigation systems apply
water to the soil slowly and steadily, directly at the
root zone, where plants need it. Because the water is

1 *Soaker hoses and drip-irrigation systems are tremendous
work- and water-savers once installed. Before installing,
prepare the soil, working in compost or other amendments.*

4 *Be sure to lay the hose so that the connecting end is on
the garden section closest to the water source.*

2 *Lay out the soaker hoses or drip lines to run around a planting area, along either side of a row, or around and between plants.*

3 *You can plant at this stage if you wish, or cover the hoses with mulch to hide them and to slow water evaporation when they are in use.*

5 *Connect the soaker hose to a conventional hose attached to an outdoor faucet or other water source.*

6 *With the irrigation system in place, you can now plant the area if you did not do so earlier.*

Watering CONTINUED

The fine foliage of love grass, Eragrostis trichodes, *holds water droplets like tiny shimmering jewels. A detail is shown above.*

applied directly to the earth, it does not dissipate in the air, and because the drip tubing is installed underground or covered by plant foliage or mulch, the moisture does not evaporate quickly.

A less sophisticated means of drip-irrigation is a soaker hose. This specially perforated hose of canvas or rubber allows water to slowly leak out along its entire length. Simply lay the hose in the area to be watered, snaking it around and among plants. Then connect it to a conventional hose that runs to the water source, and turn on the faucet at a low level. You can either retrieve the hose when you are finished, or leave it in place throughout the growing season. See pages 84–85 for step-by-step photos illustrating how to install a soaker hose.

A more high-tech version of a drip-irrigation system involves the automatically timed release of water through a perforated hose that is shallowly buried in the garden. An automatic drip-irrigation system does require an initial investment of time and money. The expenditure, however, is quickly repaid in the savings of hours spent moving and cleaning hoses and manually watering your plants.

Drip-irrigation systems are timesaving and water-saving boons for low-maintenance gardeners. Because there are so many components and products offered, however, you should probably consult a professional landscaper before installing one or, at the very least, obtain advice at a garden center or hardware store.

Weeding

*K*eeping a garden relatively weed-free may seem daunting, but you can make the chore of weeding more manageable and less frequent.

Begin any new garden with a clean slate—clear weeds before you plant by applying a low-toxicity systemic herbicide, practicing soil solarization, or manually removing all the weeds. If you use an herbicide, look for the word "glyphosphate" on the label. Products with this ingredient rarely harm animals; they kill all plants with which they come in contact within a week or so, but then quickly break down. Aim carefully when you spray the herbicide, apply it on a calm day so that the spray does not drift, wear gloves, and follow all directions on the package.

Soil solarization is only effective in areas receiving full, continual summer sun. It involves tightly covering prepared, moistened soil with clear plastic and then letting the sun bake the area for about eight weeks.

This roasting kills weeds in the covered area, but it also destroys beneficial soil microorganisms.

The most labor intensive but safest way to remove weeds is to pull them by hand. Loosen the soil with a hoe, then sift through the soil with your fingers to remove all the small weed plants.

Deter weed growth with landscape barriers and mulches. Placed just below ground level, landscape barriers consist of specially woven fabric that blocks weeds but allows water, air, and fertilizers to enter the soil. Use these barriers around newly planted shrubs.

Finally, keep an eye on the garden and pull out any weeds that do emerge while they're still small. Check your garden for stragglers during spring and fall cleanup and weekly in summer and your heavy weeding chores should be minimal. The photos on page 88 show some troublesome weeds you'll want to eliminate from your garden before you begin planting.

Without frequent removal, weeds can overrun a garden in no time. If you choose not to mulch the garden, pull the weeds when they're small; barring that, at least remove them before they go to seed.

Weeding CONTINUED

*The medicinal herb common
burdock is a troublesome
weed in many places.*

*Purple dead nettle spreads
with abandon.*

*Broad-leaved plantain is the
bane of many a lawn.*

*Chickweed has pretty little
white flowers, but is a plague
in some gardens.*

Pruning

Pruning, the removal or shortening of a woody plant's limbs, is generally undertaken for three reasons: to control the size and shape of a plant, to remove diseased and dead branches, and to increase flowering. When a tree or shrub needs regular prunings and thus regular attention, clipping can become another time-consuming garden task.

As a low-maintenance gardener, you should avoid trees and shrubs that need to be constantly pruned to look their best. Some shrubs, such as rhododendrons, never need to be pruned and are only trimmed to keep their size within bounds. Others, such as the butterfly bush *(Buddleia)*, can be cut back just once a year in the early spring to produce flowers during the growing season. These are the kinds of trees and shrubs you want for a low-maintenance garden.

Should you lose your heart to a shrub that does require periodic trimming, keep pruning to a minimum. When trimming, let the plant follow its natural growth habit. Let your forsythia, for example, grow to its natural, open form—don't try to turn it into a pompom or box. When the shrub becomes old, cut a few of the oldest stems back to the ground each year instead of shearing off the tops of all of them to control the plant's height. And never top your trees. Like shearing a flowing shrub, topping a tree makes for an awkward shape, poor growth, and few flowers. If you have to top a tree to keep it within its allotted space,

Pruning in the low-maintenance garden is kept to a minimum. Prune to remove damaged, diseased, or dead wood and to enhance a tree or shrub's natural form. The tree here maintains its graceful natural shape.

Pruning CONTINUED

TROUBLESHOOTING TIP

Never prune shrubs with dull tools. The rough cuts can rip apart stems, leaving the ragged edges vulnerable to invasion by diseases or insects. Pruning tools should also be clean. Clean your tool after each cut when you are pruning diseased limbs. Sterilize by dipping the blades into a solution of one part liquid chlorine bleach to nine parts water.

The giant dogwood (Cornus controversa) *has unusual horizontal branches arranged in tiers. It needs no pruning to assume this form, and eventually grows to 60 feet tall.*

the tree is wrong for the space. Next time choose a tree that will be smaller when it matures.

Pruning a tree or shrub to control disease, on the other hand, is a must in any kind of garden. Cut off the infected part of the plant before the disease can spread. Cut back to healthy wood, at least several inches from the site of the infection, and dip your tools in rubbing alcohol or a solution of chlorine bleach and water after each cut. If you choose dis-

ease-resistant plants initially, much of this pruning work can be eliminated.

Although a diseased branch should be removed as soon as you discover it, you can be a bit more casual when eliminating dead branches. Severe winter cold, strong winds, or heavy rains can cause otherwise healthy branches to die. Cut back these damaged branches to a living branch or bud at your convenience, but ideally when plants are dormant.

Shrubs are a marvelously low-maintenance presence in an ornamental border. When pruning a plant to increase its flowering, take into account the shrub's season of bloom. In general, spring bloomers flower on wood grown the previous year; later bloomers bear flowers that were formed on the growth of new wood in spring.

Forsythia, for example, is a spring-blooming shrub. Shortly after its cheery yellow flowers fade, next spring's buds begin to form on the new growth. If you need to prune such a shrub and still want to enjoy its flowers every spring, you need to prune immediately after flowering. That way, you are cutting off the old wood and not the new. If you prune too late you will not harm the plant, but you will cut off some of the flower buds and will as a result have fewer flowers the next spring.

Summer-flowering shrubs are best pruned in the spring. Although you can trim these plants in the fall, a spring cut eliminates the possibility that the newly shorn branches will suffer winterkill.

For the lowest maintenance of all, choose trees and shrubs that never need to be pruned, such as summer-flowering glossy abelia. Other good candidates for your easy-care garden are summer-blooming shrubs that need to be cut back only to control their size. Since the flowers bloom on new wood, you can usually give these plants a thorough crew cut, often to as low as 1 foot. See the encyclopedia section beginning on page 98 for descriptions of trees and shrubs with low-maintenance requirements.

TIMESAVING TIP

In general, evergreen shrubs —particularly conifers— shouldn't be pruned. Many simply will not make new growth after being cut back hard. It's best to lightly trim these plants once a year if you feel their appearance requires it.

Kousa dogwood (Cornus kousa) *and Chinese dogwood* (C. kousa *var.* chinensis *shown here) are resistant to the anthracnose disease that is killing so many flowering dogwoods* (Cornus florida) *in the eastern U.S.*

Pest Control

*A*ll gardeners, but particularly those interested in low-maintenance gardening, want to spend the least possible amount of time warding off mammal, bird, and insect pests in their gardens.

Integrated pest management (IPM), a new concept of controlling pests, is the compromise reached between those who want to kill every pest in sight and those who want to protect every living creature.

IPM proponents advocate using the least-toxic measures first to keep pests from destroying a garden. Chemical controls, whether plant-based substances like rotenone or synthetic pesticides such as malathion, are used only as a last resort. Low-maintenance gardeners should prevent problems in the first place rather than try to cure them.

First, do your best to create proper growing conditions for your plants. One of the basics of low-maintenance gardening is to start out by ensuring, as much as possible, good soil, proper moisture, and adequate light in the garden.

Second, choose suitable plants for your growing conditions. Delphiniums, for example, are superb for cool, moist climates but completely out of place in arid New Mexico. In drier, warmer climates you can get spikes of intense blue by planting drought-tolerant rocket larkspur *(Consolida ambigua)*.

Third, when problems arise, turn first to nonchemical controls. Unfortunately, even suitable plants placed in proper growing conditions do not always thrive. For example, native plants in their natural habitat often suffer abuse from animal pests. In the garden, you can take steps to keep these pests away. Some of these steps are discussed below.

When the first three steps prove to be ineffective, chemicals—either natural or manufactured—are used as a last resort. Under IPM, pest-specific chemicals are

1 *Bag-type traps use pheromones to lure the Japanese beetles. Set up traps well away from the plants you wish to protect, or the traps will draw more beetles into the garden.*

preferred, and they are applied in the smallest possible amounts to retard the development of immunity to the poison and to reduce harm to natural predators.

Nonchemical and chemical methods of controlling pests and disease are discussed on the following pages.

▼ Nonchemical Controls

Low-maintenance gardeners can use a wide range of nonchemical nontoxic methods—barriers, repellent plants, traps, natural predators, and cleanliness—to deter pests.

▼ Erect barriers. Fences, nets, row covers, and even selected mulches are all barriers that can be used to keep pests away from plants. You must first know your enemy before constructing a barrier. For example, a high fence is a good defense for shutting

2 *The most effective—although not the most aesthetically pleasing—way to keep deer out of the garden is to put up an 8-foot-high fence.*

3 *Once in place, this sturdy but lightweight fencing keeps deer—and rabbits—away from the garden all season long. At the end of the season, roll it up and store it.*

out deer but will do nothing to keep birds out of the blueberry bushes.

Row covers, another type of organic pest barrier, are specially woven fabrics (usually spunbonded polyester) that allow sunshine and water to pass through but block flying insects. Unfortunately, nematodes, small parasites that live in the soil, are in no way hindered by the row covers above ground.

▼ Select repellent plants. Animal pests will quickly devour some plants and avoid others at all costs.

Much has been made of using distasteful plants in warding off deer. However, what deer avoid in one area might be eaten with a vengeance in another. Also, when deer are very hungry they become less selective. There are, however, certain plants—such as daffodils, foxgloves *(Digitalis)*, and colchicums—that are poiso-

nous to deer and to many other animals. The garden predators have learned to stay away from them. Other plants, such as herbs and alliums, repel animals with their pungent odors rather than their toxic effects.

Low-maintenance gardeners can effectively use distasteful plants in two ways. You can grow *only* such plants, or you can use the plants as barriers. Thus, if you want to keep voles from burrowing into your carrots or tulips, you could try surrounding these plants with onions, garlic, or some of the more ornamental alliums.

▼ Use traps. Exercise great care if you use traps to remove pests from your garden. When used solely to capture pests (e.g., sticky yellow paper when whiteflies are present), traps can be an effective aid. When used

Pest Control CONTINUED

EARTH·WISE TIP

Toads are often a gardener's best friend. From spring through fall, they will consume thousands of insects and other pests, including cutworms, beetles, caterpillars, and slugs. Just give them a shallow pan of water in a shady spot to keep them settled on your property.

as lures, however, traps often encourage more pests than they dispose of. Japanese beetle traps and the use of beer to catch slugs are examples of traps that attract more pests than they kill.

▼ Encourage natural predators. One of the strongest arguments in favor of organic gardening methods is that there is a balance in nature in which no pest is allowed total dominance. Thus, birds feed on insects, including ladybugs, who in their turn have a well-known appetite for aphids.

Allowing natural enemies to take care of the pests in your garden is the easiest way of all. However, the results can be mixed. If there are no pests available, there will be no predators. Once a ladybug has consumed all the aphids, it will fly away—leaving an open leaf, so to speak, for the return of the aphids. Thus, there is generally some—but rarely total—pest damage

to ornamentals or crops when only biological controls are used. Some insects that are beneficial in the garden are shown below.

▼ Allow diseases to attack insects. Several insect-specific diseases keep the population growth of these pests in check. Two of these diseases have been isolated by scientists and are available commercially in a powdered form to be spread on soil. The first is *Bacillus thuringiensis*, popularly known as Bt; it is a disease that attacks the larvae of more than 60 species of moths and butterflies. The second is called milky spore disease and attacks only the grubs of Japanese beetles.

Neither disease harms humans or other animals, and both quickly degrade in sunlight. It's best to apply them to your soil on overcast days in the late afternoon or early evening.

▼ Design companion plantings. Plants have at least some degree of built-in protection against predators, particularly insects, and some plants seem to have a high degree of protection. Companion planting seeks to utilize this principle and advocates placing an insect-repelling plant next to one that is normally defenseless. For example, pungent herbs such as catnip, rosemary, sage, and basil are all supposed to repel pests. In addition, the tall large-flowered types of marigolds are touted for their pest-deterrent roots, which exude chemicals that kill nematodes.

▼ Keep your garden clean. Smaller pests, such as slugs, beetles, and cutworms love to nest in garden debris. Eggs and larvae snugly overwinter in the leaves and then emerge with the return of warm weather. You can significantly cut down on such pests by conducting a thorough fall cleanup of your garden each year and removing any diseased plants (don't put these in the compost pile) and excess leaves.

Four beneficial insects to recognize and treat kindly, clockwise from top left: tiger beetle, ladybird beetle (ladybug), green lacewing, and praying mantis.

The red-bellied woodpecker, like other woodpeckers, is an insect-eater, and a gardener's friend.

The bright feathers of the American goldfinch flash like gold in fields, meadows, and gardens. They count insects as part of their diet.

TROUBLESHOOTING TIP

Slugs have very definite dining likes and dislikes. They love to eat tender young vegetable seedlings, but are repelled by the tannin in freshly cut wood. If you mulch the border of your garden with new wood chips, few if any slugs will cross over to devour your plantings.

▼ Selected Chemical Controls

If all else fails, you can try chemical controls that are often referred to as "biorational pesticides" because they have negligible effects on humans and their surrounding environment. These are used only as a last resort because they are nonselective in their action—they can harm beneficial insects as well as pests. Insecticidal soap affords excellent control of aphids, whiteflies, and other small insects. Dusts and sprays made with plant-based poisons such as pyrethrum, rotenone, sabadilla, and nicotine are highly toxic when applied, but break down quickly when exposed to air and sunlight.

Horticultural oil sprays are effective controls for a number of pests, including borers and scale insects that attack trees and shrubs. Until recently, these sprays were applied only to dormant plants. The oil would be sprayed on trees or shrubs in early spring to smother overwintering egg masses with a nonsoluble covering.

New refining techniques, however, have led to the development of lighter oil sprays that are safe to use for insect and mite control on actively growing plants. These sprays are popularly referred to as SOS—Summer or Superior Oil Sprays. They are more highly refined than the dormant oil sprays and provide greater pesticide efficiency.

Use the dormant oil sprays in early spring before trees and shrubs end their dormant periods. Should insect pests still appear in summer, follow up with the SOS treatment.

Regional Calendar of Garden Care

 Spring

Summer

COOL CLIMATES

- Apply dormant oil spray on deciduous trees and shrubs when the temperature reaches 40°F for a 24-hour period. This must be done before growth starts. The spray will smother the egg masses of insect pests.

- Turn under green manure cover crops and work compost into the vegetable garden.

- If needed, apply lime to lawns in early spring.

- Divide crowded clumps of bulbs after they have finished flowering. Transplant extras around your property.

- Set up stakes for tall perennials before the plants grow 1 foot high.

- To prevent emergence of spring weeds, apply compost and then a thick layer of organic mulch around permanent plantings of trees and shrubs.

- Harden-off flower and vegetable seedlings grown indoors by placing them in a protected spot outdoors for 7 to 10 days before planting in full sun.

- Make sure that flowers, shrubs, and vegetables are receiving consistent, regular watering during spells of dry weather. Lawns only need to be watered deeply once a week.

- In early summer cut back fall-blooming perennials such as asters, mums, boltonia, and helenium to reduce the need for staking and to create bushier, more floriferous plants.

- Mulch open spaces in flower and vegetable gardens with organic matter to smother annual weeds, conserve moisture, and enrich the soil.

- Deadhead flowers, especially repeat bloomers. Harvest vegetables, particularly beans and squashes, that keep producing if picked.

- In late summer, plant a cover crop such as crimson clover *(Trifolium incarnatum)* or annual ryegrass *(Lolium multiflorum)* in the vegetable garden.

WARM CLIMATES

- Install a soaker hose or drip-irrigation system if they are appropriate methods of watering your garden.

- Harvest cool-season vegetable crops, and prepare the ground for planting warm-season vegetables. Rotate your plantings so that one kind of vegetable will not grow in the same spot year after year.

- Divide crowded clumps of bulbs after they have finished flowering. Transplant the extras around your property.

- Aphids and spider mites are beginning to emerge. Forcefully spray stricken plants with water or insecticidal soaps early in the morning. Taking steps now can prevent the infestation of insect populations and the need for more lethal sprays.

- If perennial ryegrass that was overseeded in winter persists in the spring, mow the lawn to less than 2 inches and reduce watering. This will encourage the bermudagrass to overtake the ryegrass.

- Be vigilant in watering spring-flowering trees and shrubs, which can become heat-stressed.

- Deadhead flowers, especially repeat bloomers. Harvest vegetables that keep producing if picked regularly, particularly beans and squashes.

- Plant heat-loving annuals such as lantana *(L. camara)*, catharanthus *(C. roseus)*, portulaca *(P. grandiflora)*, gomphrena *(G. globosa)*, and Dahlberg daisy *(Dyssodia tenuiloba)*.

- Cover berry-producing shrubs with netting when fruit starts to form.

- In late summer, clear out areas for planting a second crop of cool-season vegetables such as carrots, leaf lettuces, radishes, and spinach.

Fall

- Test soils in all areas where your plants have had trouble growing. Contact your local county cooperative extension office for information on its soil testing service.

- Check end-of-season sales at local garden centers. The savings on shrubs are usually quite generous. Examine sale plants carefully before buying.

- Clean the garden thoroughly of all leaves and spent flowers. Compost healthy plant cuttings and discard all diseased material.

- Plant hardy bulbs for care-free color next spring.

- Mulch in areas where winter snow cover is unlikely. The winter mulch helps maintain soil moisture and prevents rapid fluctuations of soil temperature, which can damage roots.

- Thoroughly clean and dry all garden tools before putting them away for the season.

- Plant maiden pinks *(Dianthus deltoides)* and pansies *(Viola spp.)* for added color throughout the winter months.

- Divide and transplant daylilies and spring-blooming perennials.

- Outbreaks of aphids, whiteflies, and leafhoppers are still possible. Be vigilant in checking plants for these pests and take immediate control measures when they appear.

- Clean the garden thoroughly of all leaves and other debris. Compost healthy plant cuttings and discard all diseased material.

- Overseed your lawn with perennial ryegrass six to eight weeks before the first heavy frost.

- Test soils in areas where your plants have had trouble. Contact your county cooperative extension office for information on soil-testing service.

🌲 *Winter*

- Winter is a good time for horticultural education. Visit flower shows, learn about new, low-maintenance plants by reading mail-order nursery catalogues, and search for good books to add to your garden library.

- Avoid using salt to melt ice near your garden beds and borders. The salt will leach into the soil and damage your plants.

- Remove heavy snow from evergreen trees and shrubs to protect branches from breaking.

- In late winter, prune fruit trees and grapevines before growth begins. Sprinkle wood ashes from your fireplace around flower beds.

- Start perennials, annuals, and vegetables from seed. This is the cheapest way to obtain plants and also the only way to grow many uncommon ones.

- Gradually remove winter mulch from garden beds after night temperatures remain above 30°F. Overcast, windless days are ideal for this task.

- Take advantage of dreary days and pursue your garden education. Visit nearby flower shows, learn about new, low-maintenance plants by reading mail-order nursery catalogues, and search for good books to add to your garden library.

- Use row covers to protect early vegetables. The covers guard against both late-season frosts and early-season bugs.

- In late winter apply nontoxic dormant oil spray to deciduous trees and shrubs when temperatures reach 40°F for a 24-hour period. This reduces scale and other insects.

- Early March is a good time to prune and plant bare-root roses and fruit and shade trees.

- Check shrubs and trees for overwintering egg masses of insect pests and promptly remove them.

This table offers a basic outline of garden care by season. The tasks for each season differ for warm and cool climates: warm climates correspond to USDA Plant Hardiness Zones 8 through 11, and cool climates to Zones 2 through 7. Obviously, there are substantial climate differences within these broad regions. To understand the specific growing conditions in your garden, consult the Zone Map on page 127. Also be sure to study local factors affecting the microclimate of your garden, such as elevation and proximity of water.

Low-Maintenance Plants

*T*his section provides concise information on more than 140 plants recommended for low-maintenance gardens. The plants have been selected on the basis of beauty, adaptability, availability, and low-maintenance requirements. None of them are finicky or difficult to grow. If you're looking for plants for particular uses—of a certain height, for instance, or with flowers of a certain color—look first at the Color Range and Growth Habit columns. If you need plants for a shady spot, look at the Growing Conditions column. Or look at the photos, read the descriptions, and then decide which plants will grow well in your garden. Each photograph shows a species or variety described in the entry.

▼ About Plant Names

Plants appear in alphabetical order by the genus name, shown in bold type (herbs and vegetables are listed by their common name). On the next line is the most widely used common name. The third line contains the complete botanical name: genus, species, and where applicable, a variety or cultivar name.

Common names vary, but botanical names are the same everywhere. If you learn botanical names, you'll always get the plant you want from a mail-order nursery or local garden center. One gardener's golden star may be another gardener's green-and-gold, but both gardeners will recognize the plant if they know its scientific name: *Chrysogonum virginianum.*

When several species in a genus are similar in appearance and cultural needs, they are listed together in a single entry in the chart. In the case of a genus containing two or more vastly different species that cannot be covered in a single entry, each of the recommended species is given a separate entry in the chart.

The second column of the chart provides a brief plant description. Look here to see if the plant is vertical, bushy, low, or creeping.

▼ Color Range

The color dots following each description indicate the color *family*, and are not a literal rendering of the flower color. A plant given a pink dot might be pale blush pink, clear pink, or bright rose pink.

▼ Time of Bloom

Bloom time is given by season and may vary from one region to another according to climate, weather, and growing conditions. For example, crocuses may bloom in February in southern gardens, but not until March or April farther north. During a cold year when spring comes late, plants will bloom later.

In warm climates a plant will generally flower in the early part of the range listed; in cooler climates it will usually bloom later. If you want more specific information on when a plant flowers in your area, ask neighbors who grow it or a local garden center or your local USDA county cooperative extension office. As you get to know your garden and its plants, you'll be able to anticipate their flowery display.

▼ Hardiness Zones

Plant hardiness is generally an indication of the coldest temperatures a plant is likely to survive. But many plants also have limits to the amount of heat they can tolerate. In this chart hardiness is expressed as a range from the coolest to the warmest zones where the plant generally thrives. The zones are based on the newest version of the USDA Plant Hardiness Zone Map, shown on page 127.

▼ Growing Conditions

The last column of the chart summarizes the best growing conditions for the plant. Look here for information on the plant's light, moisture, and soil requirements.

			Color Range	Time of Bloom	Growth Habit	Hardiness Zones	Growing Conditions
	ABRONIA HEART'S DELIGHT, SAND VERBENA *Abronia fragrans* DESERT SAND VERBENA ◂ *A. villosa*	Annuals or perennials native to Rocky Mt. foothills and Southwest. A. fragrans, a perennial, has rounded clusters of fragrant, 3/4- to 1-in. white flowers that bloom at night. A. villosa, an annual, has rosy purple flowers.	● ○ ○	Mid-spring to midsummer	Height: 6–10" Spacing: 6–12"	3 to 11	Full sun. Well-drained soil; does not tolerate soggy conditions. This perennial can be grown as an annual in many regions.
	ACER AMUR MAPLE, HEDGE MAPLE *Acer ginnala*	A large shrub or small tree that has purplish twigs, especially when young. Light yellow, fragrant flowers in spring produce reddish winged fruits in late summer. Foliage turns reddish in autumn. Short cultivars make excellent hedges.	○	Spring	Height: 3–15' Spacing: 3–15'	2 to 8	Full sun to partial shade. Well-drained, humus-rich soil with ample moisture throughout the growing season. This maple grows better in colder regions than in warm ones.
	AEGOPODIUM GOUTWEED, GROUND ELDER *Aegopodium podagraria*	A perennial that spreads rapidly from creeping root stocks. Its leaves are light green or variegated with white. It is grown more as a spreading ground cover or edging plant than for its umbels of small, relatively inconspicuous flowers.	○ ○	Late spring	Height: 6–14" Spacing: 6–12"	3 to 9	Full sun to shade. Moist soil. Keep an eye on this plant; it may become very weedy and rampant if environmental conditions are ideal.
	AESCULUS BOTTLEBRUSH, BUCKEYE *Aesculus parviflora*	A small tree or spreading shrub native to the Southeast. The compound leaves have 5 leaflets. Small white flowers are borne in dense, foot-long columns. Smooth buckeye fruits appear in late summer.	● ● ○ ○	Early summer	Height: 3–10' Spacing: 5–10'	4 to 8	Full sun to partial shade, but with some sun each day. Moist, well-drained soil that is rich in both organic matter and lime.
	AJUGA CARPET BUGLEWEED *Ajuga reptans*	A low, creeping plant that rapidly spreads from stolons. The leaves are dark, glossy green and grow to a height of only 4 in. The spikes of deep blue flowers rise up to 6 in. above the foliage. Cultivars provide color variation in leaves and flowers.	● ● ○	Spring to early summer	Height: 6–10" Spacing: 6–18"	4 to 9	Full sun to partial shade; some afternoon shade in warm climates. Plants will survive in almost any kind of soil. This ideal ground cover can become weedy if planted with other border or bedding plants.

◂ *Indicates species shown.*

Low-Maintenance Plants

			Color Range	Time of Bloom	Growth Habit	Hardiness Zones	Growing Conditions
	AMELANCHIER SHADBUSH, SERVICEBERRY ◀ *Amelanchier canadensis* *A. × grandiflora*	Compact, small trees or large shrubs with smooth, gray-striped bark. Masses of small, white flowers borne on 2- to 3-in. racemes appear early in the spring. Small (1/3-in.), red-purple, edible fruits mature in late spring.	○	Early spring	Height: 10–25' Spacing: 10–15'	3 to 8 *A. canadensis* 3 to 7 *A. × grandiflora* 4 to 8	Full sun to partial shade. Moist soil rich in organic matter, or sandy soil that never completely dries out. These shrubs may need protection from deer in winter.
	AMSONIA BLUESTAR, WILLOW AMSONIA *Amsonia tabernaemontana*	A perennial bearing dense clusters of light blue, 1/2-in., trumpet-shaped flowers with 5 long, pointed petals. They bloom on somewhat shrubby stems that arise in clumps. The willowlike leaves turn golden yellow in autumn.	●	Mid-spring to early summer	Height: 1 1/2–3' Spacing: 2–3'	3 to 9	Shade to partial sun. Moist soil. Bluestar is easy to grow, as long as the soil is not allowed to dry out. Trim back to 12 in. after flowering, unless you want pods for flower arrangements.
	ANDROPOGON BIG BLUESTEM, TURKEY-FOOT *Andropogon gerardii*	A bold, clump-forming perennial grass native to the prairies. The bluish green leaves turn bronze and red in late summer as purple flower spikes rise above the foliage. The 3-branched seed head resembles a turkey's foot.	●	Mid- to late summer	Height: 4–8' Spacing: 1 1/2–3'	4 to 10	Full sun. Well-drained, moist soil; tolerates clay soil and drought once established. Propagate by seed or by clump division in spring. Most growth occurs during the warm season.
	ANTHEMIS GOLDEN MARGUERITE *Anthemis tinctoria*	An erect to sprawling perennial with bright yellow, 1 1/2- to 2-in., daisylike flowers on branching stems. The feathery, aromatic, light turquoise-green leaves are woolly underneath. May become bushy with age.	○	Mid-spring to midsummer	Height: 2–3' Spacing: 1–1 1/2'	3 to 9	Full sun. Ordinary garden conditions or even poor, dry sites. Do not overwater. This is an excellent cutting flower, and cutting extends the flowering season. Plants can become weedy; if needed, rejuvenate plants by springtime division.
	AQUILEGIA GARDEN COLUMBINE ◀ *Aquilegia × hybrida* *A. vulgaris*	A perennial with unique flowers: five tubular petals ending in knob-tipped spurs either match or contrast the brightly colored sepals and yellow stamens. Blue-green leaves have rounded subdivisions.	●●●●○○	Spring to early summer	Height: 2–3' Spacing: 9–18"	4 to 9	Full sun to partial shade. Humus-rich, well-drained soil. Hybrid columbines tend to be short-lived and should be divided every several years. Remove leaves showing leaf-miner tunnels or stems showing borer damage.

			Color Range	Time of Bloom	Growth Habit	Hardiness Zones	Growing Conditions
	ARABIS WALL ROCK CRESS ◄ *Arabis caucasica* *A. procurrens*	A rapidly growing evergreen perennial ground cover with small clusters of white or pink, cross-shaped, $3/8$-in. flowers rising above a dense mass of gray-green foliage. Arabis looks wonderful cascading over rocks or low stone walls.	● ○	Early to mid-spring	Height: 5–10" Spacing: 6–12"	4 to 8 A. procur-rens 4 to 7	Full sun to partial shade. Well-drained to dry soil. Rock cress is an easy plant to grow in borders and rock gardens. Divide overmature plants in early spring if they show reduced flowering.
	ARTEMISIA WORMWOOD *Artemisia ludoviciana* var. *albula* ◄ *A.* × 'Powis Castle' SILVER MOUND *A. schmidtiana* 'Silver Mound'	A perennial bearing mounds of divided leaves covered with soft, silky hairs, giving the foliage a silver-green or woolly white appearance. The lacy leaves are somewhat fragrant and persist until frost. Flowers are small and gray white.	● ● ○ ○	Summer to autumn	Height: 1–3' Spacing: 1–2'	4 to 8 A. ludovi-ciana 'Silver King' 5 to 8 A. × 'Powis Castle' 5 to 8	Full sun to partial shade. Poor, dry soil. Prune occasionally to keep plants growing vigorously.
	ARUNCUS GOATSBEARD *Aruncus dioicus*	Like a large version of astilbe. Separate male and female plants both bear sprays of many small, creamy white flowers. The large compound leaves have toothed edges. Over time this perennial forms large clumps.	○	Late spring to early summer	Height: 3–6' Spacing: 3–5'	3 to 7	Full sun to partial shade. Moist, well-drained, loamy soil. If overmature plants show lack of vigor or flowering, divide the woody root stocks only in the dormant period in early spring.
	ASARUM EUROPEAN WILD GINGER *Asarum europaeum*	A rhizomatous perennial ground cover useful where winters are not severe. Glossy, evergreen, heart-shaped leaves arch over to hide 3-part, $1/2$-in., thimble-shaped maroon flowers. Root stocks smell and taste like ginger.	●	Spring	Height: 6–9" Spacing: 6–12"	5 to 9	Full to partial shade. Moist, loamy soils that never completely dry out. Easy to grow, Asarum spreads with time.
	ASCLEPIAS BUTTERFLY WEED *Asclepias tuberosa*	A spectacular native perennial that attracts butterflies into the garden. Clusters of ornate flowers range in color from yellow orange to orange to nearly red. Plants produce attractive thin pods with plumed seeds in late summer.	● ● ○ ○	Mid- to late summer	Height: $1\frac{1}{2}$–$2\frac{1}{2}$' Spacing: 6–12"	3 to 9	Full sun. Well-drained soil; does not grow or overwinter well in wet or clay soil. Seedlings may need some watering, but established plants are very drought resistant. Avoid disturbing the large tuberous rhizome; propagate from seed.

◄ Indicates species shown.

Low-Maintenance Plants

			Color Range	Time of Bloom	Growth Habit	Hardiness Zones	Growing Conditions
	ASPARAGUS GARDEN ASPARAGUS *Asparagus officinalis*	A hardy perennial vegetable whose young shoots (spears) are harvested as they emerge from the soil in the spring. When fully developed, the many-branched shoots have finely divided, 1/2-in., soft leaves. Creamy-colored flowers produce red berries.	○	*Midsummer*	Height: 3–5' Spacing: 1 1/2–2' Space rows: 3–5'	3 to 9	*Full sun. Well-drained, sandy-loam soil that never completely dries out. Plant crowns 8- to 10-in. deep in trenches. Do not harvest the first year. Provide winter mulch in regions with cold winters. Slugs or snails may be a problem.*
	ASTER NEW ENGLAND ASTER ◀ *Aster novae-angliae* NEW YORK ASTER *A. novi-belgii*	Tall, hardy perennials whose 1- to 2-in. flowers have bright golden centers. Wild forms have purple (N.E. aster) or lavender-blue (N.Y. aster) petals, but cultivars ranging from white to red are available. N.Y. aster's flowers are smaller than N.E. aster's.	●●●●●○	*Late summer to late autumn*	Height: 1–6' Spacing: 1–3'	3 to 8 A. novae-angliae 3 to 7 A. novi-belgii 4 to 8	*Full sun to light shade. Moist soil rich in organic matter. Leaves are somewhat susceptible to powdery mildew. Divide mature clumps every 3–4 years.*
	BAPTISIA BLUE FALSE INDIGO *Baptisia australis*	A native perennial that has spikes of 1-in., indigo blue, pealike flowers at the ends of stout branches. Dark leguminous pods persist into winter. The foliage is gray green. This slow-growing plant may eventually become shrublike.	●	*Late spring to midsummer*	Height: 2–5' Spacing: 2–4'	3 to 8	*Full sun to light shade. Well-drained, slightly acidic soil; does not tolerate soggy conditions.*
	BEAN BUSH BEAN *Phaseolus vulgaris* var. *humilis*	A low-growing variety of bean that assumes a bushy form rather than a trailing vine form. Many cultivars and hybrids provide a choice of pod color, texture, and maturation time.	○	*Midsummer*	Height: 8–18" Spacing: 4–6" Space rows: 1–2'	3 to 11	*Full sun. Well-drained soil; prone to fungal diseases in soggy conditions. Do not use nitrogen fertilizers; plants are nourished from nitrogen-fixing bacteria that are harmed by excess nitrogen.*
	BEET BEET *Beta vulgaris*	A biennial vegetable grown for both its bulbous taproot and for its edible leaves. Most beetroots are shades of red, but golden cultivars are available. Swiss chard is a variety grown exclusively for its leaves.	●		Height: 8–12" Spacing: 3–5" Space rows: 1–2'	3 to 11	*Full sun. Well-drained soil; does not tolerate soggy conditions. Sandy loam is best; if soil is clayey, add compost and gypsum. Too much nitrogen fertilizer causes the top leaves to grow at the expense of the roots.*

			Color Range	Time of Bloom	Growth Habit	Hardiness Zones	Growing Conditions
	BEGONIA WAX BEGONIA *Begonia × semperflorens-cultorum*	A fibrous-rooted begonia with fleshy stems, succulent, round, cupped leaves, and mounds of white, pink, or red flowers in single or double forms. The flowering season is exceptionally long. Frost-sensitive perennial often grown as an annual.	● ● ○ ● ○	*Mid-spring to early autumn*	Height: 8–12" Spacing: 6–12"	9 to 11	*Full sun to shade; some afternoon shade in warm climates. Well-drained, moist soil. In cold climates grow outdoors until fall, then cut back, put in pots, and grow inside until danger of frost has passed the next spring.*
	BERBERIS JAPANESE BARBERRY *Berberis thunbergii*	A familiar shrub used for hedges because its prickles and dense leafy branches make an effective barrier. Attractive red berries appear in autumn. There are many cultivars with leaf colors ranging from purple to yellow to variegated green.	● ○	*Mid-spring*	Height: 3–5' Spacing: 2–4'	4 to 8	*Full sun to partial shade. Not choosy about soil conditions; tolerates dry soil once established. Birds often spread the seeds far afield.*
	BETULA RIVER BIRCH, RED BIRCH *Betula nigra*	Birches are deciduous trees grown for their decorative bark. Betula nigra, a native species, has metallic red-brown bark when young; it peels with age to expose grayish or pinkish highlights. Triangular, 3-in. leaves turn yellow in autumn.	○	*Spring*	Height: 40–70' Spacing: 30'	4 to 9	*Full sun to partial shade. Humus-rich, moist, acidic soil; tolerates soggy or even dry soil once established. Do not plant in alkaline soil or add limestone as top dressing.*
	BRIZA QUAKING GRASS ◀ *Briza media* *B. minor*	A decorative clump grass with panicles of bright green, heart-shaped flowers that rise above the foliage and turn to tan in the summer. Lush, soft, foot-long leaves are evergreen and grow mostly during the cool season.	●	*Mid-spring*	Height: 1–2' Spacing: 10–15"	4 to 11 *B. minor* 7 to 11	*Full sun. Fertile soil. Provide ample moisture, especially while the grass is becoming established; thereafter it is more drought tolerant.*
	BROWALLIA BUSH VIOLET, SAPPHIRE FLOWER *Browallia speciosa*	A frost-sensitive perennial usually grown as an annual. Flowers are 1- to 2-in., 5-petaled, and usually lavender violet with white centers; blue or white cultivars are available. Lance-shaped, 4-in., light green leaves have darker veins.	● ● ● ○	*Midsummer to frost*	Height: 2–3' Spacing: 1–1½'	10 to 11	*Full sun to partial shade. Moist soil rich in organic matter. Started indoors, Browallia can be grown as an annual in colder zones; do not plant outside until all danger of frost is past. Plants can be overwintered as houseplants.*

◀ *Indicates species shown.*

Low-Maintenance Plants

		Color Range	Time of Bloom	Growth Habit	Hardiness Zones	Growing Conditions
BRUNNERA SIBERIAN BUGLOSS *Brunnera macrophylla*	Large, 8-in., attractive, heart-shaped leaves. Sprays of small, 1/4-in., sky blue flowers similar to forget-me-nots rise above the leaves and add further to the effectiveness of this perennial in shady borders.	●	Early to mid-spring	Height: 1–1 1/2' Spacing: 6–12"	3 to 8	Filtered sun to full shade; grows best with some afternoon shade in warm climates but tolerates full sun in cool climates. Well-drained soil should be evenly moist throughout the growing season. Mulch during winter in zones 3–6.
CALAMA-GROSTIS FEATHER REED GRASS *Calamagrostis acutiflora* var. *stricta* REED GRASS ◀ *C. arundinacea*	Large ornamental grasses that form clumps and produce feathery panicles of spring flowers that turn light gold by autumn. The tan foliage and seed heads remain through the winter.	○	Mid-spring	Height: 4–6' Spacing: 6–12"	5 to 9	Full sun to very light shade. Moist soil; tolerates clay soil but not drought. The root zone should be moist throughout the growing season. These are rapidly growing but noninvasive grasses.
CALLISTEMON LEMON BOTTLEBRUSH, CRIMSON BOTTLEBRUSH *Callistemon citrinus*	A shrub or tree with lance-shaped, evergreen, 3-in. leaves and dense whorls of flowers clustered at the tips of twigs. Long, bright red, 1-in. stamens give flowers the appearance of a bottlebrush. The woody fruits look like beads.	● ○	Spring to summer (periodically at other times of year)	Height: 6–20' Spacing: 6–8'	9 to 11	Full sun. Needs some moisture to get established but is quite drought tolerant thereafter. Bottlebrush is fast growing and needs severe pruning every 3 years to produce many flowers.
CALTHA MARSH MARIGOLD *Caltha palustris*	A perennial with rich yellow, 5-petaled flowers like 1- to 1 1/2-in. buttercups, borne just above bright green, rounded leaves. By early summer (after flowering) plants die back to their underground rhizomes.	○	Spring	Height: 1–2' Spacing: 1–1 1/2'	2 to 8	Full sun to partial shade. Soggy to constantly moist soil. Marsh marigold slowly spreads by self-seeding and is ideal for wetland, streamside, or bog gardens.
CAMPSIS TRUMPET CREEPER *Campsis radicans*	A deciduous native woody vine with 3-in., 5-lobed, bright red-orange (or yellow) tubular flowers and compound leaves of 7–11 leaflets. The vines climb by aerial rootlets and may eventually require additional support.	● ● ○	Midsummer to early autumn	Height: 10–40' Spacing: 1–1 1/2'	4 to 9	Full sun to light shade. Fertile soil with ample moisture. Plants need protection from winter winds in colder regions. These vines can withstand vigorous pruning.

			Color Range	Time of Bloom	Growth Habit	Hardiness Zones	Growing Conditions
	CARPINUS EUROPEAN HORNBEAM ◄ *Carpinus betulus* AMERICAN HORNBEAM *C. caroliniana*	*Small to large trees with drooping clusters of winged fruits and smooth, sinuous gray bark that resembles a flexed muscle. C. caroliniana, a native of eastern North America, is smaller than* C. betulus *and has more autumn color.*	○	*Spring*	Height: 20–50' Spacing: 15–30'	2 to 9 *C. betulus* 4 to 7	*Full sun to partial shade. Grows best in well-drained, fertile soils, but* C. caroliniana *tolerates constantly moist conditions.*
	CARROT CARROT *Daucus carota* var. *sativus*	*A biennial vegetable grown for its taproot. Many cultivars with varying characteristics are available. Harvest during the first year after the root has developed but before winter.*	○		Height: 8–12" Spacing: 3–4" Space rows: 12–15"	2 to 11	*Full sun. Well-drained, slightly acidic, sandy loam; tends to rot under soggy conditions. Carrots may be planted in early spring, but seeds are slow to germinate in cold soil.*
	CARYOPTERIS BLUEBEARD *Caryopteris × clandonensis* BLUE SPIREA ◄ *C. incana*	*Small deciduous shrubs grown for their aromatic gray-green leaves and fragrant flowers. Tubular, 1/4- to 3/8-in., violet-blue or white flowers are borne in dense clusters along the stem. C. incana is the larger of the two species.*	● ● ○	*Late summer to autumn*	Height: 2–5' Spacing: 2–4'	7 to 9	*Full sun. Well-drained soil; does not tolerate soggy conditions. Prune well after flowering stops to encourage vigorous growth during the next season.*
	CELOSIA COCKSCOMB *Celosia cristata*	*An annual grown for its elaborate, crested or feathery flower heads. Flowers are usually brilliant red or gold; cultivars are available in shades of yellow, pink, and orange. Foliage is sometimes variegated.*	● ● ● ○ ○	*Midsummer to frost*	Height: 1–2' Spacing: 6–12"	3 to 11	*Full sun to very light shade; prefers some afternoon shade in warm climates. Moist, even damp, humus-rich soils.*
	CELTIS HACKBERRY, NETTLE TREE *Celtis occidentalis*	*A handsome native tree with lopsided, lance-shaped, 4-in. leaves. The gray bark has corky ridges and thorny, warty bumps near the base of the trunk. Small flowers produce hard, dark, 1/3-in., pitted fruits that mature in autumn.*		*Mid-spring*	Height: 40–70' Spacing: 10–20'	2 to 9	*Full sun to partial shade. Prefers rich, moist soil but grows in dry, heavy, rocky or sandy soils. This rugged tree grows well even where it is dry and windy.*

◄ *Indicates species shown.*

Low-Maintenance Plants

		Color Range	Time of Bloom	Growth Habit	Hardiness Zones	Growing Conditions
CERCIS REDBUD *Cercis canadensis*	A small tree native to the southeastern U.S. that is one of the most attractive of trees, with its dense clusters of rosy pink flowers and its lustrous, deep green, heart-shaped leaves. Cultivars with white flowers or purple leaves are available.	●●	Early to mid-spring	Height: 20–30' Spacing: 10–20'	4 to 9	Full sun to light shade. Moist, well-drained soil. Redbud tolerates a wide range of conditions except constant wetness.
CHELONE TURTLEHEAD *Chelone glabra* PINK TURTLEHEAD ◀ *C. lyonii*	Native perennials whose spikes of 1-in., double-lipped flowers resemble the heads of turtles. Pairs of 5-in., clasping, lance-shaped leaves are arranged along light green stems. C. glabra has white flowers and C. lyonii *has pink ones.*	●○	Late summer to early autumn	Height: 2–4' Spacing: 9–12"	3 to 8	Full sun to partial shade. Grows best when roots are in constantly moist soil. These wetland species tolerate soil conditions ranging from those found in normal gardens to soggy, water-logged sites. Plants spread freely with age.
CHIONANTHUS FRINGE TREE *Chionanthus virginicus*	A large native shrub or small tree with showy, 6- to 8-in. clusters of feathery, fragrant white flowers that hang down below dark green deciduous leaves. Dark blue fruits are produced by autumn.	○	Spring	Height: 10–25' Spacing: 6–12'	3 to 9	Full sun to partial shade; prefers some afternoon shade in warm climates. Well-drained, fertile, slightly acidic soil that never completely dries out. Fringe tree grows slowly.
CHIONODOXA GLORY-OF-THE-SNOW *Chionodoxa luciliae*	A bulb that sends up pairs of elongated, somewhat fleshy leaves and an open, loose cluster of several light blue flowers with white centers. Cultivars are available in white or pink.	●●○	Early spring	Height: 2–6" Spacing: 1–2"	3 to 9	Full sun to partial shade. Moist, well-drained soils that are never waterlogged. Chionodoxa self-seeds and reproduces freely from offsets.
CHIVES CHIVES *Allium schoenoprasum*	A perennial herb grown for its onion-flavored, tubular leaves. It produces round clusters of lavender, 6-petaled flowers on leafless stems above clumps of foliage.	●	Late spring to mid-summer	Height: 6–12" Spacing: 1–2"	3 to 9	Full sun to partial shade. Ordinary garden soil; tolerates a wide variety of conditions. Harvest leaves as needed; they will regrow quickly. Chives make an attractive edging plant. Grow from seed or divide clumps of bulbs.

			Color Range	Time of Bloom	Growth Habit	Hardiness Zones	Growing Conditions
	CHRYSOGONUM GREEN-AND-GOLD, GOLDEN STAR *Chrysogonum virginianum*	A long-blooming perennial that makes an excellent ground cover or bedding plant. Single, bright gold composite flowers with double-pointed petals are borne on short stems above a spreading, dense mat of lustrous green leaves.	○	Early spring to mid-summer	Height: 4–8" Spacing: 6–12"	4 to 8	Full sun to medium shade; some afternoon shade in warm climates. Well-drained, moist soil. Mulch very lightly during winter in cooler climates and remove mulch early in the spring. Plants may rot if mulch is too thick.
	CIMICIFUGA BLACK SNAKEROOT ◀ *Cimicifuga racemosa* KAMCHATKA BUGBANE *C. simplex* 'White Pearl'	Bold woodland perennials with wands of small, 1/2-in., creamy white, ill-scented flowers borne on long stems. The large compound leaves are deeply lobed. C. simplex is smaller and flowers later than the native C. racemosa.	○	Midsummer to early autumn	Height: 3–6' Spacing: 1–1 1/2'	3 to 8 C. simplex 'White Pearl' 4 to 8	Dappled sun to partial shade; some afternoon shade in warm climates. Moist, well-drained soil rich in organic matter. Plants grow slowly.
	COLCHICUM AUTUMN CROCUS *Colchicum autumnale*	Perennial that sends up narrow, foot-long leaves in the spring. These die back to an underground corm during summer. Several showy, 3- to 4-in., rosy pink, purple, or white flowers appear in succession during early autumn.	●○○	Early autumn	Height: 4–6" Spacing: 4–8"	4 to 9	Full sun to partial shade. Well-drained, moist soil rich in organic matter.
	CONSOLIDA ANNUAL LARKSPUR, ROCKET LARKSPUR *Consolida ambigua*	An easy-to-grow annual that resembles the perennial larkspur. Consolida bears dense spikes of 3/4-in. flowers on stems with highly dissected leaves. Flower color ranges from white to red to purple to blue.	●●●○	Summer	Height: 1–4' Spacing: 6–12"	3 to 11	Full sun to partial shade. Fertile, well-drained soil rich in organic matter. Keep soil moist throughout the growing season. In warm regions, sow outdoors in autumn; sow in early spring elsewhere.
	CONVALLARIA LILY-OF-THE-VALLEY *Convallaria majalis*	A hardy perennial that forms a dense ground cover with attractive, spear-shaped, deep green leaves and fragrant, nodding, 1/3-in., bell-shaped white flowers.	○	Late spring	Height: 6–12" Spacing: 4–8"	3 to 8	Full to partial shade. Moist, well-drained soil rich in organic matter. With age plants form mats that should be divided and replanted to maintain vigorous growth and flowering.

◀ *Indicates species shown.*

Low-Maintenance Plants

		Color Range	Time of Bloom	Growth Habit	Hardiness Zones	Growing Conditions
COREOPSIS BIGFLOWER COREOPSIS *Coreopsis grandiflora* THREADLEAF COREOPSIS ◀ *C. verticillata* 'Moonbeam'	Easy-to-grow perennials with bright yellow flowers. C. grandiflora has 2- to 3-in. flowers and broad lance-shaped leaves. C. verticillata 'Moonbeam' has thin, wiry leaves, 1- to 2-in. flowers, and a more mounded growth form.		Late spring to late summer	Height: 1–3' Spacing: 9–12"	3 to 9 *C. grandiflora* 4 to 9	Full sun. Well-drained, moist soil. Deadhead fading flowers to prolong bloom. These are easy-to-grow perennials, although C. grandiflora is short-lived. Divide every several years to maintain vigorous growth.
CORTADERIA PAMPAS GRASS *Cortaderia selloana*	A very large, clumpy perennial grass with long, evergreen, 3/4-in.-wide leaves. Flowers grow on long shoots that rise several feet above the foliage. Female plants have much showier white or pink flower plumes than male plants.		Late summer	Height: 6–10' Spacing: 4–8'	7 to 11	Full sun. Well-drained, moist soil; withstands dry soil once established.
COTONEASTER ROCKSPRAY, ROCK COTONEASTER *Cotoneaster horizontalis*	A popular low-growing, spreading shrub whose beautiful pink flowers produce bright red, 1/3-in. berries by late summer. Small, shiny, evergreen leaves outline the horizontal sprays of branches.		Mid-spring	Height: 2–3' Spacing: 2–3'	4 to 8	Full sun to partial shade. Well-drained, moist soil rich in organic matter. Once established, plants tolerate dry soils and even windy conditions. Plants spread horizontally with age.
CRESS GARDEN CRESS, PEPPERGRASS *Lepidium sativum*	An annual herb with peppery-tasting leaves that cluster around the base of the stem and are used as a salad seasoning. Inconspicuous flowers produce elongated fruits. Cultivars with curly leaves that look like parsley are available.		Late spring to midsummer	Height: 1–2' Spacing: 2–3" Space rows: 1'	2 to 8	Full sun and ordinary garden soil conditions. Cress grows best in cool weather. Plant new seeds at monthly intervals and harvest before flowering. Plants mature in about one month.
CROCUS DUTCH CROCUS *Crocus vernus*	One of the most popular spring bulbs. Petals are typically striped or solid in color and come in yellow, white, or purple, with bright gold stamens. Striking color variants are found among the hybrids and cultivars of this old-time favorite.		Early to mid-spring	Height: 3–5" Spacing: 1–2"	3 to 8	Full sun to partial shade. Well-drained soil that is moist during the relatively short growing season and on the dry side the rest of the year. By late spring the leaves wither and die back to the underground corms.

			Color Range	Time of Bloom	Growth Habit	Hardiness Zones	Growing Conditions

DIANTHUS
DEPTFORD PINK
Dianthus armeria
MAIDEN PINK
◄ *D. deltoides*

Long-lived perennials with grass-leaved foliage and small, $1/2$- to $2/3$-in., bright pink flowers that resemble narrow-petaled sweet williams. Maiden pink blooms later and has more pronounced magenta petal stripes and wider petals.

● ● | Late spring to midsummer | Height: 6–18" / Spacing: 6–12" | 3 to 8 / *D. armeria* 4 to 8 | Full sun. Well-drained soil; does not tolerate soggy conditions. Dianthus is excellent for naturalizing in meadows and growing in rock gardens. Plants form mats with age.

DICENTRA
WILD BLEEDING-HEART
◄ *Dicentra eximia*
WESTERN BLEEDING-HEART
D. formosa

Mounds of fernlike, deeply cut leaves and erect stems bearing $3/4$-in., rose-pink flowers that look like elongated hearts. D. formosa is preferred for the West Coast and D. eximia for the East. Both have a long flowering season.

● ● | Late spring to fall | Height: 1–1$1/2$' / Spacing: 6–12" | 3 to 9 / *D. eximia* 3 to 8 / *D. formosa* 4 to 9 | Full sun to full shade; some afternoon shade in warm climates. Well-drained, moist soil. Mulch during winter in cold climates. Bleeding-heart may need to be divided if it spreads too rapidly.

DICTAMNUS
GAS PLANT
Dictamnus albus

A shrubby perennial whose 5-petaled flowers, stems, and glossy, leathery leaves have a pungent lemon-oil scent. The 1-in., white or light pink flowers have 10 showy, curved stamens.

● ○ | Late spring to early summer | Height: 1–4' / Spacing: 3–4' | 3 to 8 | Full sun to partial shade. Well-drained soil; wet soil may lead to root rot. Propagate from seeds. Gas plant does not transplant well but once established, it is long-lived and easy to care for. Plants may become shrubby with age.

DIGITALIS
YELLOW FOXGLOVE
Digitalis grandiflora
COMMON FOXGLOVE
◄ *D. purpurea*

A biennial whose rosettes of thick, soft leaves give rise to a wandlike floral shoot that bears many pink or white tubular flowers decorated with contrasting dots. D. grandiflora (also sold as D. ambigua) has yellow flowers.

○ ● ● ○ | Late spring to midsummer | Height: 2–5' / Spacing: 10–12" | 4 to 9 / *D. purpurea* 4 to 8 | Full sun to partial shade. Well-drained soil that is constantly moist. Few pests bother the leaves, the source of the drug digitalis. Plants self-seed freely, but not always where you desire them; transplant seedlings in autumn or early spring.

DIMORPHO-THECA
CAPE MARIGOLD, AFRICAN DAISY
Dimorphotheca sinuata

A frost-sensitive perennial usually grown as an annual. Daisylike flower heads have petals in pastel shades of orange, yellow, bronze, or cream. Dark bases of petals form a dramatic ring around bright gold flower centers.

● ○ ○ | Mid-spring to midsummer | Height: 6–18" / Spacing: 6–10" | 2 to 11 | Full sun. Well-drained, fertile soil; susceptible to rot and wilt if soil is too wet. To prolong flowering, remove old flowers before they set seed. Plants can be grown as winter-blooming perennials in zones 10–11.

◄ *Indicates species shown.*

Low-Maintenance Plants

		Color Range	Time of Bloom	Growth Habit	Hardiness Zones	Growing Conditions
ECHINACEA PURPLE CONEFLOWER *Echinacea purpurea*	A perennial whose coarse, rough, lance-shaped leaves grow below sturdy flower stems bearing large daisylike blooms. With dusky pink outer petals and a domed, spiny center of iridescent golden bronze, it makes an excellent cut flower.	● ● ○	Late spring to autumn	Height: 2–4' Spacing: 1–2'	3 to 8	Full sun to light shade. Well-drained, sandy-loam soil. Coneflowers are relatively drought tolerant and very easy to care for. Makes an ideal meadow plant.
EMILIA TASSEL FLOWER, FLORA'S-PAINTBRUSH *Emilia javanica*	An annual with bright yellow or red, 1/2-in., single or double, daisylike flower heads. Most of the long, narrow, grayish green foliage grows low on the stems. Blooms resemble tiny paintbrushes and make excellent cut flowers.	● ● ○	Summer	Height: 1–2' Spacing: 6–12"	3 to 11	Full sun. Well-drained soil; does not tolerate soggy conditions. Tassel flower is excellent for dry, sandy, or coastal areas. Plant seeds when danger of frost has passed. Plants are useful in dried flower arrangements.
EPIMEDIUM BISHOP'S-HAT, LONG-SPUR EPIMEDIUM *Epimedium grandiflorum* 'Violaceum'	A very durable ground cover with ornate, long-spurred, 1- to 2-in. flowers of white, red, or violet. The lush foliage is divided into groups of 6–9 heart-shaped leaflets. Foliage remains green for most of the year.	● ● ○	Late spring	Height: 8–12" Spacing: 6–12"	4 to 8	Partial to full shade. Well-drained, humus-rich soil. Once established, plants will tolerate dry conditions but do not do well in soggy soil.
ERYNGIUM ALPINE SEA-HOLLY *Eryngium alpinum*	A perennial bearing compact, 2-in., cylindrical heads of tiny, violet-blue flowers borne atop bluish stems and surrounded by feathery, blue-green, spiny leaves. White-flowered cultivars are available.	● ○	Mid- to late summer	Height: 2–2 1/2' Spacing: 1–1 1/2'	5 to 8	Full sun to partial shade. Well-drained soil; does not tolerate soggy conditions. *Eryngium* is quite drought resistant.
ESCHSCHOLZIA CALIFORNIA POPPY *Eschscholzia californica*	A short-lived perennial that can be grown as an annual just about anywhere. Poppy-like, 1- to 3-in. flowers project above ferny, grayish green leaves. The bright orange, 4-petaled, cupped flowers have golden centers.	● ○	Spring to autumn	Height: 6–18" Spacing: 6–8"	2 to 11	Full sun to partial shade. Well-drained, sandy-loam soil with low fertility. Plants frequently self-seed and can even become weedy, but a beautiful weed nonetheless. These grow as perennials in zones 9–11.

			Color Range	Time of Bloom	Growth Habit	Hardiness Zones	Growing Conditions
	EUONYMUS BURNING BUSH, WINGED SPINDLE TREE *Euonymus alata* 'Compacta'	*A leafy, deciduous shrub that turns fiery scarlet in the autumn when the orange and purple fruits appear. Twigs have 4 corky ridges, giving them the appearance of being winged.*	● ●	*Summer*	Height: 3–8' Spacing: 3–10'	4 to 9	*Full sun to partial shade. Average garden soil. Avoid waterlogged conditions.*
	EUPHORBIA SPURGE ◄ *Euphorbia characias wulfenii* CUSHION SPURGE *E. epithymoides*	*Succulent perennials bearing small flowers with visually striking short yellow or purple bracts at their bases. E. epithymoides forms cushion-shaped flowers that turn reddish in autumn. E. characias wulfenii is more erect and has thicker stems.*	● ○	*Mid-spring to early summer*	Height: 1–3' Spacing: 1½–2'	4 to 11 E. characias wulfenii 7 to 11 E. epithy- moides 4 to 9	*Full sun to very light shade. Well-drained soil.*
	FELICIA BLUE MARGUERITE *Felicia amelloides* KINGFISHER DAISY ◄ *F. bergerana*	*Among the most elegant of plants, with daisylike, 1-in. flowers with sky blue outer petals and bright yellow centers. F. amelloides is a small, frost-sensitive ever-green shrub. F. bergerana is an annual.*	● ○ ○ ○	*Late spring to autumn*	Height: 6–18" Spacing: 6–12"	3 to 11	*Full sun. Well-drained soil. Avoid wet situations. Grow both species as annuals; F. amelloides can be grown as a perennial in zones 10–11.*
	FESTUCA BLUE FESCUE, SHEEP FESCUE *Festuca ovina* var. *glauca*	*A low, tufted grass with light bluish green leaves. Short spikes of flowers grow above the clumps of foliage. Festuca makes an attractive edging plant but does not withstand foot traffic. This fescue is sometimes listed as F. cinerea.*	○ ○	*Spring to early summer*	Height: 4–12" Spacing: 6–8"	4 to 9	*Full sun to partial shade. Moist, well-drained soil. Plants grow slowly or become dormant during hot, dry periods. In hot regions plant in partial shade and provide supplemental water. Cut back the tops in autumn.*
	FILIPENDULA QUEEN-OF-THE- PRAIRIE ◄ *Filipendula rubra* QUEEN-OF-THE- MEADOW *F. ulmaria*	*A graceful perennial bearing beautiful, foamy clusters of tiny, light pink, 5-petaled flowers on long stems that also bear bold, deeply lobed, angular leaves. Cultivars with deeper red flowers are available. Flowers of F. ulmaria are white.*	● ○ ● ○	*Early to mid-summer*	Height: 4–6' Spacing: 1–2'	3 to 9 F. ulmaria 4 to 9	*Full sun to light shade. Well-drained, evenly moist soil rich in organic matter, but will thrive even in wet soil. Native F. rubra and its Asian relative F. ulmaria are ideal for wet meadows and prairies.*

◄ *Indicates species shown.*

Low-Maintenance Plants

			Color Range	Time of Bloom	Growth Habit	Hardiness Zones	Growing Conditions
	FORSYTHIA FORSYTHIA, BORDER FORSYTHIA *Forsythia × intermedia*	A very popular deciduous shrub with clusters of bright yellow, 1- to 2-in. flowers in spring followed by lustrous green, toothed, lance-shaped leaves. Many cultivars of this hybrid vary in flower and leaf forms and in growth habit.	○	Mid-spring	Height: 5–10' Spacing: 6–12'	4 to 8	Full sun to partial shade. Moist, well-drained soil, but tolerates a wide range of conditions. Mulch during winter and protect from winter winds in colder climates.
	FRAXINUS EUROPEAN ASH *Fraxinus excelsior*	A large tree with stout twigs bearing black buds and pairs of compound leaves, each with 7–11 leaflets. In silhouette, the tree has a rounded crown, although some of the many cultivars have flattened tops.		Spring	Height: 70–80' Spacing: 25–50'	4 to 8	Full sun to partial shade. Moist soil rich in organic matter and limestone. European ash is susceptible to insect pests (especially ash borer).
	GAILLARDIA BLANKET FLOWER *Gaillardia aristata* ◀ *G. × grandiflora* 'Goblin'	Excellent flowering perennials for borders or meadows. The hybrid 'Goblin' has bright scarlet, daisylike flowers with yellow, toothed tips. Somewhat domed flower centers may be scarlet, maroon, or yellow.	● ● ○	Summer	Height: 1½–2' Spacing: 1–1½'	3 to 9	Full sun. Well-drained soil. In wet soil plants become leggy and prone to rotting during winter. Do not fertilize; gaillardia does best in nutrient-poor soil with little organic matter.
	GALIUM SWEET WOODRUFF *Galium odoratum*	An easy-to-grow, perennial ground cover also used to flavor wines. Lance-shaped 1- to 2-in. leaves are arranged around the square stems in whorls of 6–8. Cross-shaped, ¼-in., white flowers are borne in loose clusters above the foliage.	○	Spring	Height: 8–12" Spacing: 6–12"	4 to 8	Partial shade. Well-drained, evenly moist soil. Sweet woodruff may spread too rapidly and become weedy in sites with abundant organic matter and moisture.
	GARLIC GARLIC *Allium sativum*	A perennial, bulb-producing herb grown for its aromatic cloves, which are covered in white, papery skins. Flat, grasslike leaves clasp the tough stem, which bears a cluster of small white flowers.	○	Summer	Height: 1½–2' Spacing: 5–6" Space rows: 1½–2'	6 to 8	Full sun. Moderately moist, well-drained soil not too rich in nutrients. If the soil is too fertile, most of the growth goes into the tops rather than the cloves.

			Color Range	Time of Bloom	Growth Habit	Hardiness Zones	Growing Conditions
GERANIUM LILAC CRANESBILL *Geranium himalayense* ◀ G. × 'Johnson's Blue' BLOOD-RED CRANESBILL *G. sanguineum*		Hardy perennials that form mounds of 5-lobed, dissected, deep green leaves. All 3 species have showy, 5-petaled flowers; G. sanguineum has deep magenta flowers while 'Johnson's Blue' and G. himalayense have violet-blue flowers.	● ●	Late spring to early fall	Height: 8–18" Spacing: 1–1¹/₂'	3 to 8 G. × 'Johnson's Blue' 4 to 8 G. sanguineum 4 to 8	Full sun to partial shade; some afternoon shade in warm climates. Well-drained, moist soil rich in organic matter.
GINKGO GINKGO, MAIDENHAIR TREE *Ginkgo biloba*		A medium to tall tree with a strongly pyramidal crown. Light green, fan-shaped leaves turn golden yellow in the autumn. Since female trees produce bad-smelling fruits, select the male tree for planting.		Spring	Height: 50–80' Spacing: 2¹/₂–5'	3 to 9	Full sun. Well-drained, moist soil. These trees adapt to a wide variety of environmental conditions.
GLEDITSIA HONEY LOCUST *Gleditsia triacanthos* var. *inermis*		A large, bold tree whose 6- to 8-in., doubly compound leaves have about a hundred leaflets. Pendant clusters of small yellowish green flowers produce flattened, brown 8- to 18-in. pods. This honey locust lacks the thorns of other varieties.	●	Late spring to early summer	Height: 30–70' Spacing: 20–30'	3 to 9	Full sun. Moist, well-drained soil rich in organic matter and limestone. Honey locust is drought tolerant once established and adaptable to a wide variety of conditions.
HAMAMELIS WITCH HAZEL *Hamamelis* × *intermedia*		A deciduous shrub available in many cultivars. Plants are a hybrid of Japanese and Chinese species and flower from late January to mid-March, depending on the cultivar. Colors of flowers and fall leaves vary from yellow to red.	● ○	Winter to early spring	Height: 15–20' Spacing: 6–12'	5 to 8	Full sun to partial shade. Moist, well-drained, slightly acidic soil rich in organic matter. Witch hazel is generally susceptible to serious diseases or insect pests.
HEDERA ENGLISH IVY *Hedera helix*		An evergreen perennial with lustrous, leathery leaves. Many cultivars vary in degree of leaf dissection, leaf variegation, and hardiness. Grows outdoors as a ground cover or vine or as a houseplant.		Mid-autumn	Height: 3"–30' Spacing: 1–1¹/₂'	4 to 9	Full sun to shade; some afternoon shade in warm climates. Moist, well-drained, humus-rich soil in a wide range of acidity. Select hardy cultivars such as 'Bulgaria' for cold regions.

◀ *Indicates species shown.*

Low-Maintenance Plants

		Color Range	Time of Bloom	Growth Habit	Hardiness Zones	Growing Conditions
HELIANTHEMUM SUN ROSE, ROCK ROSE *Helianthemum nummularium*	A shrubby, low, spreading evergreen perennial with pairs of narrow, grayish leaves and clear yellow, pink, or orange, 5-petaled flowers on slender stems.		Early summer	Height: 8–12" Spacing: 6–12"	6 to 8	Full sun. Well-drained, lime-rich soil; does not tolerate soggy conditions. Prune back after flowering to stimulate new, vigorous growth. Mulch during winter in cooler climates.
HEMEROCALLIS ORANGE DAYLILY *Hemerocallis fulva* LEMON DAYLILY ◄ *H. hybrids* *H. lilioasphodelus*	A perennial with 3- to 4-in. flowers that last but a day. Numerous buds give these plants a long season of bloom. Many hybrids and cultivars provide a staggering array of pure and mixed colors from reds through yellows.		Late spring to summer	Height: 1–5' Spacing: 1½–2'	3 to 9	Full sun to light shade; some afternoon shade in warm climates. Well-drained soil rich in organic matter. Roots and root stocks enlarge with age and need to be divided periodically. Slugs and snails can be a problem.
HEUCHERA CORALBELLS, ALUMROOT *Heuchera × brizoides* ◄ *H. sanguinea*	A perennial composed of mounded mats of glossy, round-lobed, evergreen leaves that are attractive throughout the year. Clusters of small, cup-shaped, pink, red, or white flowers are borne on leafless, wandlike stems.		Late spring to late summer	Height: 1–2' Spacing: 1–1½'	3 to 8 *H. × brizoides* 4 to 8	Partial shade to full sun. Well-drained, moist, humus-rich soil. These natives are ideal for rock gardens; they tend to rot under soggy conditions.
HOSTA HOSTA, PLANTAIN LILY ◄ *Hosta fortunei* *H. sieboldiana* FRAGRANT PLANTAIN LILY *H. plantaginea*	A long-time favorite perennial for shade gardens. Hostas combine various shades of green or variegated foliage with spikes of pastel lavender, blue, or white flowers. Species, hybrids, and cultivars vary in size, shape, and flower color.		Early summer to fall	Height: 1–3' Spacing: 1–2'	3 to 8	Full sun to shade. Well-drained, moist soil; prone to rotting if soil is not well drained. Plants grow in shade, partial shade, or even full sun if the soil is sufficiently moist. Mulch during winter in cold climates. Slugs and deer may be a problem.
IBERIS EVERGREEN CANDY-TUFT *Iberis sempervirens*	A creeping perennial ideal for rock gardens or hanging baskets. Clusters of showy, small, bright white flowers nearly obscure mats of 1½-in., narrow, deep green leaves.		Early to mid-spring	Height: 6–12" Spacing: 1–1½'	3 to 9	Full sun to very light shade. Well-drained, humus-rich soil. Prune after flowering to promote reblooming and more vigorous growth. Mulch during winter in cold climates.

			Color Range	Time of Bloom	Growth Habit	Hardiness Zones	Growing Conditions
	IBERIS ANNUAL CANDYTUFT, GLOBE CANDYTUFT *Iberis umbellata*	*A popular edging or border annual with dense clusters of 4-petaled, 1/2-in. flowers in white, pink, red, or violet. Leaves are lance-shaped and dark green. Some cultivars offer bicolored flowers.*		Summer to early autumn	Height: 6–12" Spacing: 5–8"	3 to 11	Full sun. Well-drained soil. Candytuft grows vigorously and continues to flower nearly until frost.
	IMPATIENS IMPATIENS, GARDEN BALSAM *Impatiens balsamina* ZANZIBAR BALSAM ◄ *I. wallerana*	*Tender bedding plants used for their showy 1- to 2-in., soft-petaled flowers. Colors of single or double-flowered hybrids include white, pink, peach, yellow, or even dark red. Bicolored forms are also available.*		Late spring to frost	Height: 6–18" Spacing: 6–12"	2 to 11	Filtered sun to partial shade. Fertile, well-drained soil with ample moisture. Start plants indoors in cold regions and set outside after danger of frost has passed. Grow both species as annuals in zone 10.
	IRIS SIBERIAN IRIS *Iris sibirica*	*Showy 2- to 3-in. blue, purple, red, yellow, or white flowers borne on strong leafless stems. These perennial rhizomatous plants arise as long, saberlike leaves that grow in compact clumps. Many cultivars are available in varying colors and sizes.*		Late spring to midsummer	Height: 1–3' Spacing: 1–2'	3 to 8	Full sun to partial shade. Normal, well-drained, moist garden soil. These colorful plants are easy to grow.
	JUNIPERUS CHINESE JUNIPER *Juniperus chinensis*	*An evergreen conifer available in cultivars that range in size from shrubs to large trees. The flat needles come in two forms, one with sharp points and the other with rounded tips. Male and female cones are borne on separate plants.*		Spring	Height: 3–60' Spacing: 3–20'	3 to 9	Full sun to partial shade. Does not tolerate soggy conditions. Junipers may be troubled by slugs and snails and are also susceptible to juniper blight.
	JUNIPERUS CREEPING JUNIPER *Juniperus horizontalis*	*A low, creeping, evergreen shrub that forms a mat. Dense, spiny or scaly, light blue-green leaves mostly cover the branches. Tiny cones produce a 1/3-in., waxy, blueberry-like fruit. Many cultivars are available.*		Spring	Height: 10–24" Spacing: 1–2'	3 to 9	Full sun. Any soil except those that are soggy. Extreme conditions, such as drought or waterlogged soil, make plants susceptible to juniper blight. Plants slowly spread with age to form sprawling mats.

◄ *Indicates species shown.*

Low-Maintenance Plants

			Color Range	Time of Bloom	Growth Habit	Hardiness Zones	Growing Conditions
	KOELERIA JUNE GRASS *Koeleria cristata*	A medium-sized bunch grass native to North American prairies. This grass grows in clumps of light green, 1/4-in.-wide leaf blades. The compact, 6-in., wandlike panicle of tiny flowers tapers toward the tip.	● ○	*Late spring*	Height: 1–2' Spacing: 6–8"	2 to 8	*Full sun to partial shade. Well-drained soil that is moist when seedlings or divisions are becoming established. Thereafter Koeleria is quite drought tolerant. Do not add fertilizer, as June grass thrives in nutrient-poor soils.*
	LATHYRUS PERENNIAL PEA *Lathyrus latifolius*	A climbing perennial vine that bears clusters of 1- to 2-in., pealike flowers in white, pink, red, or lavender. The flowers lack the fragrance of sweet peas (L. odoratus), *but* L. latifolius *grows more vigorously.*	● ● ● ● ○	*Midsummer to early autumn*	Height: 4–8' Spacing: 1½–2½'	4 to 9	*Full sun. Well-drained, moist soil; prone to mildew and rotting if soil is too wet. Support this climber with a stone wall, fence, or trellis. Remove withering blossoms to promote further flowering.*
	LETTUCE GARDEN LETTUCE *Lactuca sativa*	A cool-season annual vegetable whose leaves are used as salad greens. There are many easily grown, leafy (not forming a tight head) hybrids and cultivars in colors ranging from green to red and with broad to deeply lobed leaves.	○	*Late summer*	Height: 6–12" Spacing: 5–8" Space rows: 1–1½'	2 to 9	*Full sun to very light shade; some afternoon shade in warm climates. Well-drained soil that never completely dries out. In warm regions, grow as a winter crop. Harvest before flowers are produced and leaves become bitter.*
	LIATRIS GAY-FEATHER *Liatris pycnostachya* SPIKE GAY-FEATHER ◄ *L. spicata*	A native perennial bearing small, rosy lavender, shaggy flowers clustered in tight heads that bloom from the top down on 1- to 2-ft. stems. The lower halves of the stems are covered with attractive, grasslike leaves.	● ●	*Midsummer to early autumn*	Height: 1–2½' Spacing: 6–12"	3 to 9	*Full sun. Well-drained, moist soil rich in organic matter. Divide clumps if flowering decreases with time.*
	LILIUM ASIATIC HYBRID LILY ◄ *Lilium 'Enchantment'* TIGER LILY *L. lancifolium*	Perennial bulbs producing several to many large (5-in.), 6-petaled, orange flowers on tall stems. Tiger lily is taller and has purple spots on its dangling flowers. 'Enchantment' blooms earlier.	●	*Early summer to early autumn*	Height: 2–5' Spacing: 6–12"	3 to 9 *L. 'Enchantment'* 3 to 8	*Full sun to partial shade. Moist, fertile, well-drained soil. Do not allow soil to dry out during growing season. L. 'Enchantment' is better than L. lancifolium for warm regions. Divide bulbs when plants become crowded.*

			Color Range	Time of Bloom	Growth Habit	Hardiness Zones	Growing Conditions
	LOBULARIA SWEET ALYSSUM *Lobularia maritima*	An easy-to-grow but frost-sensitive perennial usually grown as a hardy annual. Plants form dense mounds of petite, 4-petaled, white, lavender, pink, or violet flowers. The masses of flowers cover the small green leaves.	● ● ● ○	*Late spring to frost*	Height: 1–2' Spacing: 6–8"	2 to 11	*Full sun to light shade. Well-drained, moist garden soil. Shear plants after first wave of flowering to prolong bloom. Plants can be grown as winter annuals (or perennials) in warm regions.*
	LONICERA TRUMPET HONEY-SUCKLE *Lonicera sempervirens*	A native woody vine that is evergreen in warm regions but deciduous farther north. Red-orange, tubular, 2-in. flowers with yellow throats are this plant's main attraction. Scarlet- and yellow-flowered cultivars are available.	● ● ●	*Summer*	Height: 4–8' Spacing: 1½–2½'	4 to 11	*Full sun to partial shade. Likes moist soil but tolerates a wide variety of conditions. Plants can be grown as a sprawling, shrubby ground cover or trained to climb on fences or a trellis. Prune periodically if growth becomes too rampant.*
	MISCANTHUS MAIDEN GRASS *Miscanthus sinensis* 'Gracillimus' ZEBRA GRASS ◀*M. sinensis* 'Zebrinus'	Large ornamental grasses that form clumps of foliage from which rise bold 1- to 1½-ft. panicles of flowers. Seed heads remain through the winter. Zebra grass has yellow bands across the green leaves.	● ● ● ●	*Early to mid-autumn*	Height: 6–12" Spacing: 5–8" Space rows: 1–1½'	5 to 9	*Full sun. Moist, fertile, well-drained soil. As both species of grasses grow, they may need dividing to maintain their shape.*
	MUSCARI GRAPE HYACINTH *Muscari armeniacum*	A popular springtime bulb. Clumps of grassy 9-in. leaves appear in the autumn and remain green through the winter. In the spring, grapelike clusters of blue flowers bloom on leafless stalks that rise above the leaves.	●	*Early spring*	Height: 1–5' Spacing: 6–12"	2 to 9	*Full sun. Moist, well-drained, fertile soil. If flowering decreases with time, divide the bulbs during the summer when they are dormant.*
	MYRICA BAYBERRY *Myrica pensylvanica*	A small to medium-sized, deciduous shrub grown mostly for its aromatic, 1/4-in., blue-gray berries, used to scent bayberry candles. The leathery, spatula-shaped leaves are also fragrant. Male and female plants are needed to produce berries.	●	*Spring*	Height: 2–5' Spacing: 6–12"	3 to 9	*Full sun. Grows best in sandy loam but tolerates a wide variety of soil conditions. This coastal native is quite tolerant of salt and wind. In colder regions it is deciduous, but it often retains leaves where winters are mild.*

◀ *Indicates species shown.*

Low-Maintenance Plants

		Color Range	Time of Bloom	Growth Habit	Hardiness Zones	Growing Conditions
NARCISSUS NARCISSUS, DAFFODIL *Narcissus* species and hybrids ◄ *N. pseudonarcissus* *N. triandrus* 'Thalia'	Among the most beloved of the springtime bulbs. There are hundreds of daffodil cultivars and hybrids to choose from. N. pseudonarcissus has sulphur yellow solitary flowers. 'Thalia' has clusters of several white flowers.	● ○ ○	Early to mid-spring	Height: 8–18" Spacing: 6–12"	3 to 9	Full sun to semishade. Well-drained, fertile soil kept moist during spring flowering season. Do not trim back leaves until they have turned brown and withered. Some Narcissus types are good for naturalizing. Divide when too dense.
NEMOPHILA BABY-BLUE-EYES *Nemophila menziesii*	A rapidly growing annual bearing many 1- to 1½-in., cupped flowers with 5 petals that are sky blue at the tips and white-streaked with blue at the bases. The stems and soft, hairy leaves of this California native tend to sprawl along the ground.	● ○	Late winter to mid-spring	Height: 10–20" Spacing: 6–12"	2 to 11	Full sun to partial shade. Well-drained soil that is moist but not wet while the plants are in flower. Plants are easy to grow from seed; plant in autumn in zones 9–11 and in early spring elsewhere.
OENOTHERA SUNDROPS *Oenothera fruticosa*	A native perennial of the Southeast. This day-flowering evening primrose has many bright yellow, 4-petaled, 1½- to 2-in. flowers. Each flower lasts only a day, but the flowering season is relatively long.	○	Late spring to midsummer	Height: 1½–2' Spacing: 6–12"	4 to 8	Full sun to partial shade; some afternoon shade in warm climates. Moist, well-drained soil rich in organic matter.
ONION ONION *Allium cepa*	Popular vegetable grown for its pungent bulbs and sometimes its hollow, succulent green stems. Plants produce round clusters of white, ¼-in. flowers. Cultivars range from shallots to Bermuda onions to top onions with aerial bulbs.	○	Late summer	Height: 1–4' Spacing: 6–12"	3 to 10	Full sun. Well-drained soil; does not tolerate soggy conditions. Raise from seeds or small bulbs ("sets"). When tops start to yellow, break the stems over and allow to wither. Dig up bulbs before ground freezes.
OXYDENDRUM SOURWOOD *Oxydendrum arboreum*	A medium-sized deciduous tree with branches that droop toward the tips and a narrowly pyramidal crown. Drooping, 8-in. clusters of fragrant, white, bell-shaped flowers produce brown pods that last through the winter.	○	Midsummer	Height: 25–30' Spacing: 15–25'	6 to 9	Full sun or partial shade. Well-drained, moist soils that are rich in organic matter. Sourwood grows best in slightly acidic soil.

			Color Range	Time of Bloom	Growth Habit	Hardiness Zones	Growing Conditions
	PACHYSANDRA PACHYSANDRA, JAPANESE SPURGE *Pachysandra terminalis*	A slow-spreading, low ground cover with whorls of dark, lustrous evergreen leaves. Plants produce short spikes of creamy white flowers after the new leaves appear in spring. Cultivars are available with variegated leaves.	○	Early spring to early summer	Height: 6–12" Spacing: 6–12"	3 to 8	Full sun to deep shade; needs some afternoon shade in warm climates. Well-drained, moist, fertile soils with ample organic matter. In all climates, partial shade produces the best growth.
	PANICUM SWITCH GRASS *Panicum virgatum*	A versatile bunch-forming grass native to North American prairies. Tall stems bear 1- to 2-ft. green blades that turn yellow in the autumn. Tall, loose panicles of small reddish flowers persist into winter. Many cultivars are available.	● ●	Midsummer	Height: 4–6' Spacing: 10–20"	5 to 9	Grows best in full sun and moist, fertile soil but tolerates a wide variety of soil conditions. Switch grass is very tolerant of wind and salt spray.
	PARSLEY PARSLEY *Petroselinum crispum*	A biennial herb grown as an annual in the garden or as a pot herb for its deep green, pungent foliage. Several varieties differ in the amount of leaf curliness; some produce edible roots.	○	Midsummer	Height: 6–12" Spacing: 6–8"	2 to 11	Full sun to partial shade. Moist, well-drained soil of average fertility. Grow as an annual. Soak seeds in water overnight to hasten germination. Harvest leaves by picking them rather than by uprooting plants. Can be brought indoors for winter.
	PARTHENO-CISSUS BOSTON IVY *Parthenocissus tricuspidata*	A woody vine usually grown on the side of a building as a vertical wall covering and climbing by means of tendrils with small pads. The deciduous, 3-lobed leaves turn brilliant red in autumn. Plants produce attractive, 1/4-in., dark blue berries.	○ ○	Midsummer	Height: 10–50' Spacing: 6–12'	4 to 8	Full sun to partial shade; some afternoon shade in warm climates. Not at all choosy about soil conditions. With time the climbing tendrils may contribute to the erosion of masonry joints. Vines may need pruning around windows.
	PEA GARDEN PEA ◄ *Pisum sativum* SNOW PEA *P. sativum* var. *macrocarpon*	Annual vegetables grown for their moist seeds or, as with snow pea, their edible pods. Most varieties are tender vines that climb by tendrils, but dwarf, bushy cultivars are available. The flowers are typically white.	○	Late spring to early summer	Height: 3–6' Spacing: 3–4" Space rows: 2–3"	2 to 9	Full sun to partial shade. Well-drained, moist soil. Peas grow best in cool weather. Provide supports or mesh netting for tall varieties to grow upon. Do not provide additional nitrogen fertilizer.

◄ Indicates species shown.

Low-Maintenance Plants

		Color Range	Time of Bloom	Growth Habit	Hardiness Zones	Growing Conditions
PENNISETUM FOUNTAIN GRASS *Pennisetum setaceum*	A narrow-leaved perennial grass that grows in clumps. Flowering shoots overarch the foliage and bear feathery, cylindrical, pinkish flower clusters that resemble a small fountain.		Late spring to early summer	Height: 1–2' Spacing: 1–1¼'	8 to 11	Full sun. Well-drained soil. This grass seems to thrive on neglect but is sensitive to frost. It tends to become weedy in warm, dry regions, spreading by seeds.
PHALARIS RIBBON GRASS *Phalaris arundinacea* 'Picta'	An ornamental perennial grass whose spreading shoots and towering spikes of soft, white flowers add drama to garden borders. Broad, ¾- to 1-in. leaf blades are variegated with creamy white edges. Phalaris is an excellent ground cover.		Late spring	Height: 2–4' Spacing: 6–12"	4 to 9	Partial sun to partial shade; afternoon shade in warm climates. Moist soil; will even grow in waterlogged soils.
PHORMIUM NEW ZEALAND FLAX *Phormium tenax* 'Tricolor'	A large perennial for warm-climate gardens with plenty of space. Striking sword-shaped, 5-in.-wide leaves with red-orange lines on their margins grow up to 9 ft. long. The dull red flowers grow in clusters above the center of the foliage.		Summer	Height: 8–10' Spacing: 5–10'	9 to 11	Full sun to light shade. Prefers well-drained soil. This fast-growing plant is not at all fussy and can withstand periodically wet soils or drought. It is prone to root rot if soil is wet for prolonged periods.
PHYSOSTEGIA OBEDIENT PLANT, FALSE DRAGONHEAD *Physostegia virginiana*	A good perennial for borders or wildflower meadows. Lance-shaped, deep green leaves clasp square stems that are topped by conical spires of shell pink, rose, or lavender, tubular, 2-lipped flowers. White cultivars are available.		Late summer to early autumn	Height: 2–4' Spacing: 1–1½'	3 to 8	Full sun to partial shade; needs shade in warm climates. Average soil conditions; tolerates relatively nutrient-poor or damp soils.
PLATYCODON BALLOON FLOWER *Platycodon grandiflorus*	A showy perennial that gets its name from balloon-shaped flower buds that open into 3-in., cupped blue flowers with 5-pointed lobes. Varieties and cultivars come with white or pink flowers. Stems often benefit from staking.		Midsummer	Height: 1–3' Spacing: 1–1¼'	3 to 8	Full sun and well-drained soil with ample moisture throughout the growing season. Mulch during winter in cold climates.

			Color Range	Time of Bloom	Growth Habit	Hardiness Zones	Growing Conditions
	POLEMONIUM GREEK VALERIAN, JACOB'S-LADDER *Polemonium caeruleum* ◀ *P. reptans*	Perennials native to the eastern U.S. Attractive, ladderlike leaves grow on the lower half of long stems that bear loose clusters of bell-shaped, blue (or sometimes white), 1/2-in. flowers. P. reptans is smaller and grows to about 1 ft.	● ○	Late spring to late summer	Height: 8–30" Spacing: 8–12"	2 to 8 P. caeruleum 2 to 7	Full sun to partial shade. Well-drained soil that is evenly moist and rich in humus. Mulch during winter in cold climates.
	POLYGONATUM SOLOMON'S-SEAL *Polygonatum biflorum* FRAGRANT SOLOMON'S-SEAL ◀ *P. odoratum*	Perennials grown for the visual appeal of their 1/3-in., blue black berries as much as for the 3/4-in., pale green, tubular flowers dangling below arching stems. P. odoratum has fragrant flowers and comes in a variegated cultivar.	●	Spring	Height: 1–21/2' Spacing: 1–11/4'	3 to 9 P. biflorum 5 to 7	Partial sun to full shade. Well-drained soil rich in organic matter and evenly moist throughout the growing season. Polygonatum may be troubled by slugs and snails.
	POLYGONUM CHINA FLEECE VINE, SILVER LACE VINE *Polygonum aubertii*	A twining, deciduous perennial vine with 2- to 3-in., lance-shaped leaves and erect clusters of fragrant, 1/4-in., white flowers. Flowers produce pink, 3-angled fruits.	○	Summer to autumn	Height: 20–30' Spacing: 6–12"	5 to 9	Full sun to partial shade. Dry to moist soil. Silver lace vine is a vigorous grower that can become weedy with time; plants easily withstand heavy pruning.
	PORTULACA PORTULACA, ROSE MOSS *Portulaca grandiflora*	A slow-growing annual ground cover or edging plant with brightly colored, bowl-shaped flowers in yellow, orange, pink, white, and magenta, blooming all summer long. The spreading, succulent stems bear fleshy, lance-shaped leaves.	● ● ○ ◐ ○	Summer to early autumn	Height: 6–8" Spacing: 6–8"	3 to 11	Full sun. Average, well-drained soil. Portulaca is easy to grow. In cold regions, start plants indoors in flats and transplant when all danger of frost has passed.
	PULMONARIA LUNGWORT, JERUSALEM SAGE ◀ *Pulmonaria officinalis* BETHLEHEM SAGE *P. saccharata*	A perennial with attractive mottled, hairy leaves and 5-petaled flowers held above the foliage. P. officinalis has white or red flowers. P. saccharata has blue flowers that turn pink with age.	● ● ◐ ○	Spring	Height: 8–18" Spacing: 6–12"	3 to 8	Full to partial shade. Moist, humus-rich soil; does not grow well in dry conditions. Pulmonarias may need periodic division to stimulate vigorous blooming. Slugs and snails can be a problem.

◀ Indicates species shown.

Low-Maintenance Plants

		Color Range	Time of Bloom	Growth Habit	Hardiness Zones	Growing Conditions
RADISH RADISH *Raphanus sativus*	One of the easiest and fastest-growing annual vegetables, cultivated for its crisp, fleshy, pungent taproot. Rough leaves grow in a clumped rosette until the flower-bearing shoot bolts and displays yellow, 4-petaled flowers.	●	Spring to autumn	Height: 6–12" Spacing: 2–3"	2 to 11	Full sun. Moist, well-drained soil of moderate fertility. Sow seeds at frequent intervals and harvest before flowering, as soon as taproots attain full size. Many cultivars varying in root characteristics are available.
RHUS WINGED SUMAC, SHINING SUMAC *Rhus copallina* SMOOTH SUMAC ◀ *R. glabra*	Small native trees or large shrubs with smooth, stout twigs bearing 6- to 12-in., toothed, compound leaves. R. copallina has more lustrous leaves and leaflets connected by a leafy "wing." Both species turn bright red in autumn.		Late spring to midsummer	Height: 10–20' Spacing: 6–12'	2 to 9 R. copallina 4 to 9	Full sun to partial shade. These species are not particular about conditions as long as soil is well drained. Trees spread by root suckers; with time they may become somewhat weedy.
ROSA RUGOSA ROSE, SALTSPRAY ROSE *Rosa rugosa*	Old-fashioned, shrubby rose with leathery deciduous foliage and a succession of large (3¹/2-in.), 5-petaled, fragrant magenta flowers with bright gold centers. Produces large, ovoid fruits (hips). White- and pink-flowered cultivars are also available.	● ● ○ ○	Early summer to early autumn	Height: 3–6' Spacing: 1–3'	4 to 9	Full sun to light shade. Well-drained soil with ample moisture and organic matter. R. rugosa tolerates windy and salty environments and is one of the best roses for seaside plantings.
RUDBECKIA BLACK-EYED SUSAN *Rudbeckia hirta* GLORIOSA DAISY ◀ *R. hirta* 'Gloriosa Daisy'	A native perennial that is usually grown as an annual. The 2-in., daisylike flowers have deep yellow outer petals and domed, silky, deep brown centers. The cultivar 'Gloriosa Daisy' is larger and has outer petals banded with dark red.	● ● ●	Midsummer to early autumn	Height: 1–2' Spacing: 9–15"	3 to 9	Full sun to very light shade. Well-drained, average garden soil. R. hirta is a short-lived perennial, but it reseeds well. Plants may become weedy in the garden but are ideal for wildflower meadows.
RUDBECKIA BLACK-EYED SUSAN *Rudbeckia fulgida*	Similar to R. hirta, *but larger (approaching shrubby), more floriferous, and later blooming. This long-lived perennial produces 2- to 2¹/2-in. flower heads of deep yellow with domed brown centers.*	● ○	Midsummer to mid-autumn	Height: 2–3' Spacing: 1¹/2–2'	3 to 9	Full sun to partial shade; some afternoon shade in warm climates. Moist, well-drained soil. R. fulgida is long blooming and forms rapidly spreading clumps in light soil.

			Color Range	Time of Bloom	Growth Habit	Hardiness Zones	Growing Conditions
	SALVIA MEALY-CUP SAGE ◄ *Salvia farinacea* SCARLET SAGE *S. splendens*	Ornamental sages grown as annual bedding plants for their showy clusters of 2-lipped flowers. S. farinacea *is larger and more branching, and has white or blue flowers.* S. splendens *is more compact and has bright scarlet flowers.*	● ● ● ○	Summer to frost	Height: 1–4' Spacing: 6–12"	9 to 11	Full sun to partial shade. Well-drained, moist soil. These frost-sensitive perennials are tough and adaptable and can be grown as annuals almost anywhere.
	SCILLA SIBERIAN SQUILL *Scilla siberica*	An excellent spring bulb for naturalizing. Small spikes of bright blue, 6-petaled, 1/2-in. flowers dangle from single stems rising above small clusters of 6-in., fleshy, basal leaves. Cultivars with white or streaked blue flowers are available.	● ○	Early spring	Height: 3–6" Spacing: 2–3"	1 to 8	Full sun to partial shade. Well-drained soil of average fertility. Squill spreads rapidly by self-sowing and bulb offsets.
	SEDUM STONECROP ◄ *Sedum 'Autumn Joy'* *S. spectabile*	A perennial with lush, succulent leaves that have notched or wavy-toothed edges. Small, 5-petaled, red or pink flowers are borne in dense clusters above leafy stems. 'Autumn Joy' has pink flowers that deepen to copper bronze.	● ● ●	Late summer to autumn	Height: 6–24" Spacing: 6–12"	3 to 8	Full sun to partial shade. Well-drained, humus-rich soil. This drought-resistant plant thrives even if neglected.
	SEMPERVIVUM HEN-AND-CHICKENS, HOUSELEEK *Sempervivum tectorum*	A succulent perennial with flat evergreen leaves arranged in a 3- to 4-in. rosette. The pointed leaves are often purple-tipped. Clusters of purple-red flowers grow on a stem that rises a foot above the foliage.	●	Early to mid-summer	Height: 3–6" Spacing: 4–8"	5 to 9	Full sun. Well-drained soil; does not tolerate soggy conditions and is quite drought resistant. Plants need little care. An excellent plant for rock gardens, S. tectorum *is also effective as a slow-growing ground cover or even a houseplant.*
	SENECIO DUSTY-MILLER *Senecio cineraria*	A frost-sensitive perennial grown as an annual. Its silver-white, deeply cut leaves are more attractive than its small clusters of rounded, yellow, daisy-like flowers. The plant sometimes grows into a small shrub.	●	Midsummer	Height: 8–24" Spacing: 8–18"	9 to 11	Full sun to very light shade. Well-drained soil; does not tolerate soggy conditions. Dusty-miller is usually grown as an annual in regions colder than zone 9.

◄ *Indicates species shown.*

Low-Maintenance Plants

		Color Range	Time of Bloom	Growth Habit	Hardiness Zones	Growing Conditions
SHALLOT SHALLOT *Allium cepa*	Small, mildly flavored onions grown for both their bulbs and their pungent, hollow leaves (used like scallions or chives). Rounded clusters of violet, 6-petaled flowers bloom on tops of leafless stems. Also sold as A. ascalonicum.	●	Midsummer	Height: 1–1½' Spacing: 6–8"	3 to 11	Full sun. Well-drained, moist soil rich in organic matter. Shallots are prone to rot in wet soil. Grow these perennials as annuals, digging them up and allowing them to dry when the tops start to turn tan.
SILENE SEA CAMPION *Silene vulgaris* subsp. maritima	A spreading perennial that forms tufted mats. Trailing stems bear pairs of lance-shaped, gray-green leaves and clusters of white, 5-petaled flowers with green inflated bases. Pink and double-flowered cultivars are available.	◗ ○	Late spring to midsummer	Height: 8–12" Spacing: 6–12"	4 to 8	Full sun. Well-drained, sandy-loam soil. Grows well under average garden conditions. Makes an excellent rock garden or seaside plant because it tolerates drought and salt.
SPIRAEA BUMALD SPIREA *Spiraea × bumalda* 'Anthony Waterer' S. japonica BRIDAL-WREATH ◀ S. × vanhouttei	Deciduous shrubs with fine twigs and compact form. They bear many clusters of small, 5-petaled flowers that look like miniature roses. S. japonica has pink flowers that bloom later in the season than the white flowers of bridal-wreath.	◗ ○	Late spring to late summer	Height: 2–6' Spacing: 2–6'	3 to 8	Full sun to light shade. Moist, fertile, well-drained soil; will adapt to most conditions as long as moisture is available.
SPOROBOLUS NORTHERN DROPSEED *Sporobolus heterolepis*	A perennial grass native to the tallgrass prairies. Long, light green, arching, ⅛-in.-wide blades form dense, lush tufts. Hummocks turn golden as autumn approaches. Showy flowers form loose clusters above the foliage.	◗ ○	Midsummer	Height: 1–3' Spacing: 1–1½'	3 to 9	Full sun. Well-drained soil that is dry and rocky. Dropseed grows well in a wide range of soil conditions as long as drainage is good. Once established, it is quite tolerant of heat and drought.
STACHYS LAMB'S-EARS *Stachys byzantina* 'Silver Carpet'	A slowly creeping perennial that forms dense clumps with age. The soft, woolly leaves are the most striking feature. The small, purple, 2-lipped flowers are themselves rather inconspicuous, but are produced on tall, stout stems.	● ○ ◗ ○	Late spring to midsummer	Height: 6–18" Spacing: 6–12"	4 to 8	Full sun to partial shade. Needs well-drained soil; tends to rot under soggy conditions. Mulch during winter in cooler climates.

		Color Range	Time of Bloom	Growth Habit	Hardiness Zones	Growing Conditions
THALICTRUM MEADOW RUE *Thalictrum delavayi* ◀ *T. rochebrunianum*	Graceful perennials that form clumps of tall shoots bearing delicate, rounded, compound leaves and loose panicles of puffy flowers. T. delavayi *has lavender flowers with yellow centers, and* T. rochebrunianum *has white, pink, or lilac flowers.*	● ● ○	Mid- to late summer	Height: 2–5' Spacing: 8–18"	4 to 9 T. delavayi 5 to 9 T. rochebrunianum 4 to 8	Full sun to partial shade. Well-drained, fertile, moist soil.
THYME THYME *Thymus vulgaris*	A shrubby perennial whose aromatic, gray-green foliage is used as a culinary herb. It has tiny oval, evergreen leaves and loose clusters of lilac flowers.	●	Summer	Height: 6–12" Spacing: 6–12"	4 to 11	Full sun. Well-drained soil of average fertility. In regions colder than zone 6, the limit of its frost hardiness, treat thyme as an annual.
TORENIA BLUEWINGS, WISHBONE FLOWER *Torenia fournieri*	An annual bearing unusual, 5-petaled flowers with dark blue-purple wing markings at their flaring tips. The throat of the flower is light lavender with a yellow blotch on the lowest petal.	● ○ ○	Midsummer to early autumn	Height: 6–12" Spacing: 6–8"	3 to 11	Partial shade. Well-drained, moist, fertile soil. This fast-growing yet frost-sensitive annual should be started indoors in all regions north of zone 10. Transplant outdoors after soil has warmed and danger of frost has passed.
TRADESCANTIA SPIDERWORT ◀ *Tradescantia* × *andersoniana* WIDOW'S TEARS *T. virginiana*	Native eastern U.S. perennial and its hybrid. The deep blue, 3-petaled flowers with golden anthers last only one day, but each stem bears many buds. The 8-in. blue-green leaves clasp slightly fleshy stems. Hybrids come in many flower colors.	● ● ○	Midspring to midsummer	Height: 1–2½' Spacing: 6–12"	4 to 9	Full sun to shade. Well-drained, fertile, moist soil. Plants will tolerate a wide range of conditions. With abundant moisture, nutrients, and sun, they may need dividing every year to keep them under control.
VERONICA SPEEDWELL, VERONICA ◀ *Veronica longifolia* *V. spicata*	Two herbaceous perennials bearing conical spikes of small, blue, tubular flowers. V. longifolia *has a profusion of deep blue flowers.* V. spicata *has gray-green leaves and has white- and rose-flowered cultivars as well as blue ones.*	● ● ○	Late spring to midsummer	Height: 1–4' Spacing: 6–12"	4 to 8	Full sun to partial shade. Well-drained, moist soil for optimum growth. Mulch during winter in cold climates.

◀ *Indicates species shown.*

Low-Maintenance Plants

		Color Range	Time of Bloom	Growth Habit	Hardiness Zones	Growing Conditions
VIBURNUM VIBURNUM *Virburnum × burkwoodii* *V. × juddii* ◀ *V. plicatum*	Attractive deciduous shrubs bearing showy clusters of small flowers in spring. The pairs of dark green leaves turn reddish in autumn. V. × burkwoodii *has fragrant pink flowers, while* V. × juddii *and* V. plicatum *have white flowers.*	● ○	Mid- to late spring	Height: 7–10' Spacing: 5–10'	4 to 9 *V. × burk-woodii* 4 to 8 *V. × juddii* 5 to 9 *V. plicatum* 5 to 8	Full sun to partial shade. Well-drained, moist, and fertile soil. Avoid water-logged sites; viburnums are prone to rotting and disease if drainage is inadequate.
VINCA PERIWINKLE, VINCA *Vinca minor*	One of the most easily grown evergreen perennial ground covers. Vinca *species have thin, sprawling stems with pairs of glossy, leathery, dark green leaves. Lavender-blue, 5-petaled flowers grow singly above the mat of foliage.*	● ○	Mid-spring to early summer	Height: 4–6" Spacing: 10–12"	4 to 8	Full sun to shade; some afternoon shade in warm cli-mates. Grows well in any type of soil, provided it doesn't dry out completely.
VIOLA SWEET VIOLET *Viola odorata*	A perennial with attractive heart-shaped leaves and fra-grant, 5-petaled flowers in purple, blue, or white. In warm regions its leaves may remain green during winter.	● ● ○	Spring	Height: 4–12" Spacing: 6–12"	6 to 9	Full sun to partial shade. Moist, humus-rich soil. Sweet violets slowly creep by rhizome growth or self-seeding. Under ideal growing conditions they may become rampant.
YUCCA ADAM'S-NEEDLE *Yucca filamentosa* SOAPWEED ◀ *Y. glauca*	Native perennials that form clumps of tough, spine-tipped, 2-ft.-long, swordlike leaves. A branched stalk bearing many waxy white, 2-in., pendant flowers arises from the mass of leaves.	○	Summer	Height: 5–12' Spacing: 3–6'	3 to 11 *Y. glauca* 4 to 11	Full sun to partial shade. Well-drained soil. These drought-tolerant plants do not tolerate soggy condi-tions. The plant center dies after flowering, but offsets will flourish. Mulch Adam's-needle during winter in colder climates.
ZELKOVA JAPANESE ZELKOVA *Zelkova serrata*	A medium-sized, deciduous tree with a spreading crown. The sharp-toothed, elmlike leaves turn from deep green to deep golden orange in autumn. The gray bark, smooth at first, becomes cracked with age.		Early spring	Height: 50–75' Spacing: 20–40'	5 to 8	Full sun to light shade. Moist, deep soil. Trees need moisture to become estab-lished, but thereafter they are quite tolerant of drought and wind.

Plant Hardiness Zone Map

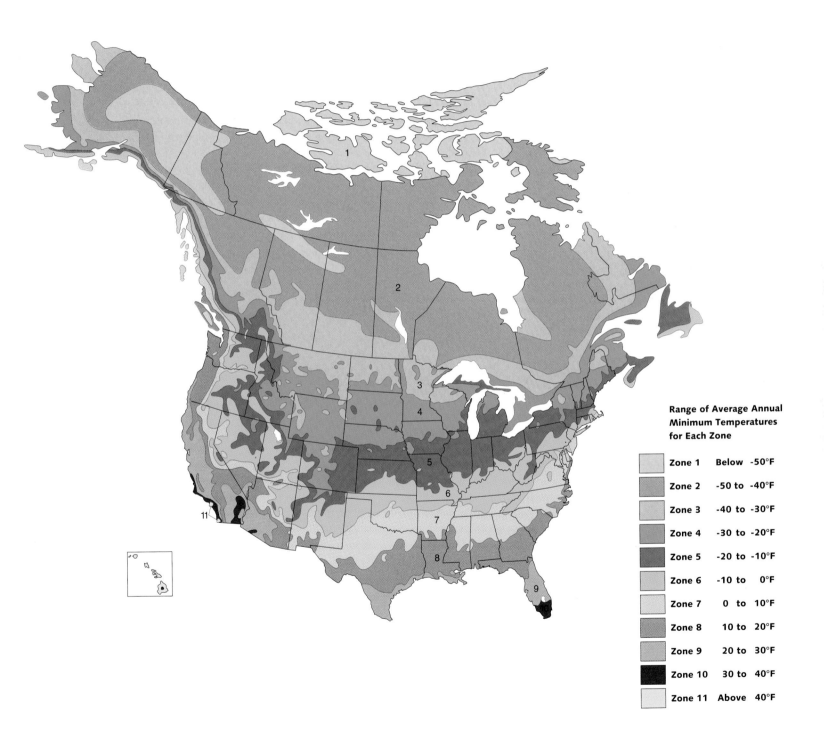

Range of Average Annual Minimum Temperatures for Each Zone

Zone 1	Below	-50°F
Zone 2	-50 to	-40°F
Zone 3	-40 to	-30°F
Zone 4	-30 to	-20°F
Zone 5	-20 to	-10°F
Zone 6	-10 to	0°F
Zone 7	0 to	10°F
Zone 8	10 to	20°F
Zone 9	20 to	30°F
Zone 10	30 to	40°F
Zone 11	Above	40°F

Resources for Low-Maintenance Gardens

There are many dependable mail-order suppliers that can be helpful for gardeners interested in saving time or energy. A selection is included here. Most have catalogues available upon request (some charge a fee). For further information and supplier suggestions, *The Complete Guide to Gardening by Mail* is available from the Mailorder Association of Nurseries, Department SCI, 8683 Doves Fly Way, Laurel, MD 20783. Please enclose $1.00 for postage and handling in the United States ($1.50 for Canada).

Plants and Seeds

W. Atlee Burpee & Co.
300 Park Avenue
Warminster, PA 18974
215-674-4900
Seeds and supplies from one of the oldest names in American gardening.

Bluestone Perennials
7211 Middle Ridge Road
Madison, OH 44057
800-852-5243
Sells perennials and selected shrubs, ornamental grasses, ferns.

Greenlee Nursery
301 E. Franklin Avenue
Pomona, CA 91766
909-629-9045
Catalogue features ornamental grasses, sedges, and rushes.

Gurney's Seed & Nursery Co.
110 Capital Street
Yankton, SD 57078
605-665-1930
Seeds, plants, and fertilizers for flower and vegetable gardeners.

Holbrook Farm & Nursery
P.O. Box 368
115 Lance Road
Fletcher, NC 28732
704-891-7790
Specializes in perennials, wildflowers, and selected trees and shrubs.

Jackson & Perkins
2518 S. Pacific Highway
Medford, OR 97501
800-292-4769
Though known for roses, they also sell perennials, trees, shrubs, and garden ornaments.

Klehm Nursery
4210 North Duncan Road
Champaign, IL 61821
800-553-3715
Grows and sells peonies, daylilies, hostas, grasses, ferns, and many other perennials.

Logee's Greenhouses
141 North Street
Danielson, CT 06239
203-774-8038
Catalogue features dozens of varieties of begonias, also ferns, fancy-leaved geraniums, tropicals, and rare plants.

Milaeger's Gardens
4838 Douglas Avenue
Racine, WI 53402-2498
800-669-9956
Over 300 varieties of perennials, including grasses and vines.

Park Seed Co.
Cokesbury Road
Greenwood, SC 29647
800-845-3369
Catalogue offers seeds, plants, bulbs, tools, and a wide selection of gardening supplies.

Seed Savers Exchange
3076 North Winn Road
Decorah, IA 52101
319-382-5990
Non-profit organization with publication for its members who want to save and exchange seeds of heirloom fruits and vetetables.

Shady Oaks Nursery
112 10th Avenue S.E.
Waseca, MN 56093
507-835-5033
Good selection of plants that grow well in shade, including hosta, wildflowers, and ferns.

Spring Hill Nurseries
6523 N. Galena Road
Peoria, IL 61632
800-582-8527
Plants and bulbs, specializing in perennials, shrubs, ground covers, and roses.

Stokes Seeds, Inc.
Box 548
Buffalo, NY 14240-0548
716-695-6980
Flower and vegetable seeds and supplies for commercial farmers and home gardeners.

Thompson & Morgan
P.O. Box 1308
Jackson, NJ 08527-0308
800-274-7333
Seeds of all types and a wide range of other garden supplies.

André Viette
Route 1, Box 16
Fishersville, VA 22939
703-943-2315
Specializes in perennials, including daylilies, hostas, and ornamental grasses.

Wayside Gardens
1 Garden Lane
Hodges, SC 29695
800-845-1124
Sophisticated ornamental plants, including many hard-to-find perennials.

White Flower Farm
Route 63
Litchfield, CT 06759
203-496-9624
Shrubs, perennials, supplies, books, gifts.
Particularly beautiful
color catalogue.

Regional Specialties

Abbey Gardens
4620 Carpinteria Avenue
Carpinteria, CA 93013
805-684-5112
Specializes in cacti and
succulents.

Kurt Bluemel, Inc.
2740 Greene Lane
Baldwin, MD 21013
410-557-7229
Specializes in ornamental
grasses, sedges, and
rushes as well as perennials, bamboos, ferns, and
aquatic plants

Busse Gardens
13579 10th Street N.W.
Cokato, MN 55321-3601
612-286-2654
Catalogue features cold-
hardy and hard-to-find
perennials.

Hastings
2350 Cheshire Bridge
Road N.E.
Atlanta, GA 30324
404-321-6981

Heirloom flowers and
shrubs, disease-resistant
and easy-to-grow flowers
selected for the Southeast.
High Altitude Gardens
P.O. Box 1048
Hailey, ID 83333
208-788-4363
Seeds selected for their
ability to grow at high
altitudes.

Ed Hume Seeds, Inc.
P.O. Box 1450
Kent, WA 98035
206-859-1110
Untreated flower, herb,
and vegetable seeds for
short-season climates.

Seeds Blum
Idaho City Stage
Boise, ID 83706
208-342-0858
Sells vegetables, annuals,
and perennials for various
conditions.

Specialty Tools

Alsto's Handy Helpers
P.O. Box 1267
Galesburg, IL 61401
800-447-0048
Offers a selection of easy-
to-use tools as well as
classic garden furniture,
container plants, and gift
items.

Gardener's Eden
P.O. Box 7307
San Francisco, CA 94120
800-822-9600
Many items appropriate
for gardeners, including
outdoor containers, tools,
and accessories.

Gardener's Supply Co.
128 Intervale Road
Burlington, VT 05401
800-876-5520
Innovative gardening
products including gifts
and accessories, green-
house kits, composting
equipment, and irrigation
needs. Call for individual
catalogues.

Plow & Hearth
P.O. Box 830
Orange, VA 22960
800-866-6072
Gardening tools and
products as well as garden
ornaments and furniture.

Smith & Hawken
P.O. Box 6900
Florence, KY 41022
800-776-3336
Well-crafted tools as well
as containers, supplies,
and furniture.

Solutions
P.O. Box 6878
Portland, OR 97228
800-342-9988
Offers home and gar-
dening products designed
to make jobs easier.

Supplies and Accessories

Gardens Alive!
5100 Schenley Place
Lawrenceburg, IN 47025
812-537-8650
Beneficial insects and a
complete line of supplies
for organic gardening.

Garden Way, Inc.
102nd St. & 9th Ave.
Troy, NY 12180
800-833-6990
Mowers, rototillers,
garden carts, and various
other lawn and garden
equipment.

Home Gardener
Manufacturing Company
30 Wright Avenue
Lititz, PA 17543
800-880-2345
Composting and related
gardening equipment.

Kemp Company
160 Koser Rd.
Lititz, PA 17543
800-441-5367
Features shredders, chip-
pers, and other power
equipment.

Kinsman Company
River Road
Point Pleasant, PA 18950
800-733-5613
Fine quality tools and
equipment. Known for
black steel modular
arches that are easy to set
up and maintain, plus
many gardening gift
items.

The Lawn Institute
Homeowner's Resource
Guide, Dept. BHG
1509 Johnson Ferry
Road, N.E., Suite 190
Marietta, GA 30062
Offers brochures on
planting, watering, and
fertilizing your lawn, and
grass seed selection for
your area. Send a self-
addressed stamped enve-
lope to receive an order
form for the brochures.

Mantis
1028 Street Road
Southampton, PA 18966
800-366-6268
215-355-9700
Lawn and garden equip-
ment, including tillers and
chippers.

Necessary Trading Co.
691 Salem Avenue
New Castle, VA 24127
800-447-5350
Catalogue includes insec-
ticidal soaps, beneficial
insects, botanicals, fertilizers, mechanical pest
controls, and other nat-
ural products.

Ringer Corporation
9959 Valley View Road
Eden Prairie, MN 55344
612-941-4180
Organic soil amendments,
beneficial insects, garden
tools, and irrigation
equipment.

Index

Numbers in boldface type indicate illustrations

A

Abelia, Glossy *(Abelia)*, 89, 90
Abronia, 99, **99**
Acer, 26, 36, 56, 59, **59**, 99, **99**
Adam's-needle, 126
Aegopodium, 19, 99, **99**
Aesculus, 46, **46-47**, 99, **99**
Ageratum, Hardy, 12, 65
Ajuga, 17, 22, 99, **99**
Alfalfa, 72, 81
Allium, **14**, 67, 71, 93, 106, **106**, 112, **112**, 118, **118**, 124, **124**
Alumroot, 114, **114**
Alyssum, Sweet, 117, **117**
Amelanchier, 42, 56, 58, 100, **100**
Amsonia, Willow *(Amsonia)*, 100, **100**
Andropogon, 100, **100**
Annuals, 63-65
Anthemis, 46, **46-47**, 100, **100**
Aquilegia, **14**, 80, 100, **100**
Arabis, 101, **101**
Arborvitae, 6, 43, **43**, 57
Artemisia *(Artemisia)*, 48, 49, **48-49**, 101, **101**
Aruncus, 101, **101**
Asarum, 16, 19, 22, 101, **101**
Asclepias, 36, 101, **101**
Ash, European, 112, **112**
Ashes, wood, 13, 76, 77, **77**
Asparagus, Garden *(Asparagus)*, 52, **52-53**, 73, 102, **102**
Aster *(Aster)*, 102, **102**
  New England, 102, **102**
  New York, 102
Azalea, 6, **17**, 23, 24, 58

B

Baby-blue-eyes, 118, **118**
Balloon Flower, 120, **120**

Balsam
  Garden, 115
  Zanzibar, 115, **115**
Baptisia, 17, 102, **102**
Barberry, Japanese, 103, **103**
Barriers, 41-43, **42**, **43**, 87, 92-93
Basil, 28, 53, 94
Bayberry, 117, **117**
Bean, 29, 73, **73**, 81, 82, 102, **102**
  Bush, 102, **102**
Beefsteak plant, 26, **26**, 64
Beet, 14, 52, **52-53**, 82, 102, **102**
Begonia, Wax *(Begonia)*, 48, 49, **48-49**, 64, **65**, 66, 103, **103**
Berberis, 103, **103**
Bermudagrass, 22, **22**
Beta, 102, **102**
Betula, 56, 59, 103, **103**
Birch
  Red, 103, **103**
  River, 56, 59, 103, **103**
Bishop's-hat, 110, **110**
Black-eyed Susan, 14, 36, 122, **122**
Blanket Flower, 36, 112, **112**
Bleeding-heart
  Western, 109
  Wild, **14**, 60, 109, **109**
Bluebeard, 105
Bluegrass, Kentucky, 68
Bluestar, 100, **100**
Bluestem, Big, 100, **100**
Bluewings, 125, **125**
Borders, 23-25, **23**, **24**, **25**
Bottlebrush, 99, **99**
  Crimson, 104, **104**
  Lemon, 18, 104, **104**
Bridal-wreath, 57, 124, **124**
Briza, 103, **103**
Broccoli, 29, 82
Browallia, 103, **103**
Brunnera, 26, 104, **104**

Buckeye, 99, **99**
  Bottlebrush, 46, **46-47**
Buddleia, 24, 89
Buffalo Grass, 35
Bugbane, Kamchatka, 107
Bugleweed, Carpet, 17, 22, 99, **99**
Bugloss, Siberian, 26, 104, **104**
Bulbs, 18, 66-67
Burning Bush, 24, 111, **111**
Butterfly Bush, 24, 89
Butterfly Weed, 36, 101, **101**

C

Cabbage, 73, **73**, 82
Calamagrostis, 36, 21, **21**, 68, 104, **104**
Calendar of garden care (regional), 96-97
Callistemon, 104, **104**
Caltha, 38, 104, **104**
Campion, Sea, 124, **124**
Campsis, 12, 36, 104, **104**
Candytuft
  Annual, 52, **52-53**, 115, **115**
  Evergreen, 36, 114, **114**
  Globe, 115, **115**
Carpinus, 105, **105**
Carrot, **28**, 52, 53, 93, 105, **105**
Caryopteris, 46, **46-47**, 57, **57**, 105, **105**
Celosia *(Celosia)*, 105, **105**
  Castle Pink, 64
Celtis, 36, 105, **105**
Cercis, 106, **106**
Chelone, 106, **106**
China Fleece Vine, 121, **121**
Chionanthus, 49, **48-49**, 56, 106, **106**
Chionodoxa, 46, **46-47**, 106, **106**
Chives, 28, 52, **52-53**, 70, 71, **71**, 80, 106, **106**
  Garlic, 71

Chrysogonum, 17, 98, 107, 107
Cimicifuga, 107, **107**
Cistus, **14**, 17
Climate and hardiness, 16-17
Clover, 20, 72, 96
Cockscomb, 105, **105**
Colchicum *(Colchicum)*, 66, 67, 93, 107, **107**
Columbine, Garden, **14**, 80, 100, **100**
Compost, 12, 25, 28, 33, 40, 48, 78-79, **77**, 83, **83**, 84
Coneflower, Purple, 61, **61**, 110, **110**
Conifers, 57, 91
Consolida, 36, 92, 107, **107**
Container gardens, 34, 42
Convallaria 27, **27**, 48-49, 49, 107, **107**
Cool-climate plants, 16
Coralbells, 27, 50, **50-51**, 114, **114**
Coreopsis *(Coreopsis)*, 50, **50-51**, 108, **108**
  Bigflower, 108
  Moonbeam, 27, 41, 60, 108, **108**
  Threadleaf, 50, **50-51**, 108, **108**
Cornus, 16, 24, 58, **58**, 59, **59**, 90, **90**, 91, **91**
Cortaderia, 108, **108**
Cotoneaster, Rock *(Cotoneaster)*, 36, 108, **108**
Cranesbill, 21
  Blood-red, 113
  Lilac, 50, **50-51**, 113, **113**
Cress, 28, 108, **108**
  Garden, 108, **108**
  Wall Rock, 101, **101**
Crocus *(Crocus)*, 18, 66, 82, 98, 108, **108**
  Dutch, 108, **108**

Crocus, Autumn *(Colchicum)*, 66, 67, 107, **107**
Crop rotation, 81-82

D

Daffodil, 66, **66**, 67, 93, 118, **118**
Daisy
  African, 109, **109**
  Gloriosa, 122
  Kingfisher, 111, **111**
Daucus, 105, **105**
Daylily, 48, **48-49**, 49, 60, **60**, 97
  Lemon, 114, **114**
  Orange, 114
Dianthus, 97, 109, **109**
Dicentra, **14**, 60, 109, **109**
Dictamnus, 109, **109**
Digitalis, 62, **62**, 93, 109, **109**
Dimorphotheca, 109, **109**
Dogwood, 16, 23-24, 58, **58**, 91
  Chinese, 59, **59**, 91, **91**
  Giant, 59, 90, **90**
Dragonhead, False, 120, **120**
Drainage pipes and tiles, 15, 34, 38, 39, **39**
Drainage problems, 15, 32-40, 84-86
Drip-irrigation systems, 34, 84-85, **84-85**, 86
Dropseed, Northern, 124, **124**
Drought-tolerant gardens, 32-36, **33**
Dry conditions, 32-36
Dusty-miller, 123, **123**

E

Echinacea, 61, **61**, 110, **110**
Edgings, 21, **21**, 31, **31**
Emilia, 110, **110**
Encyclopedia of low-maintenance plants, 98-126
Epimedium, Long-spur *(Epimedium)*, 110, **110**

Eryngium, 110, **110**
Eschscholzia, 52, **52-53**, 110, **110**
Euonymus, 24, 26, 111, **111**
Euphorbia, 36, 64, 111, **111**

F
Feather Reed Grass, 36, 68, 104
Felicia, 111, **111**
Fertilizer, 12, 22, 63, 76, 78, 79
Fescue *(Festuca)*
  Blue, 36, 111, **111**
  Fine, 68
  Sheep, 111, **111**
  Tall, 20, **20**, 68
Filipendula, **41**, 111, **111**
Flax, New Zealand, 120, **120**
Flora's-paintbrush, 110, **110**
Foliage, 26-27, **26**, **27**, 64, **64**, 84
Forsythia *(Forsythia),* 46, **46-47**, 89, 91, 112, **112**
  Border, 112, **112**
Fountain Grass, 120, **120**
Foxglove, 62, **62**, 93
  Common, 109, **109**
  Yellow, 109
Fraxinus, 112, **112**
Fringe Tree, 49, **48-49**, 56, 106, **106**

G
Gaillardia, 36, 112, **112**
Galium, 19, 112, **112**
Garlic, 52, 53, **53**, 70, **80**, 93, 112, **112**
  Daffodil, 67
Gas Plant, 109, **109**
Gay-feather, 116
  Spike, 116, **116**
Geranium *(Geranium),* **21**, 50, **50-51**, 113, **113**
  Lancaster, 60
Geranium *(Pelargonium),* 32, 64, **65**
Ginger, 22, 65
  Canada Wild, 16, 19
  European Wild, 101, **101**
Ginkgo *(Ginkgo),* 113, **113**
Gleditsia, 36, 59, 113, **113**
Glory-of-the-snow, 46, **46-47**, 106, **106**
Goatsbeard, 101, **101**

Golden Star, 17, 98, 107, **107**
Goutweed, 19, 99, **99**
Grass
  Lawn, 20, **20**, 22, **22**, 35, 68, 96, 97
  Ornamental, **6**, 7, **7**, 68-69, **68**, **69**, 78, **78**, 79, **79** (see also individual plant names)
  Green-and-gold, 98, 107, **107**
Ground cover, 19-22, **19**, **20**, **21**, 34
Ground Elder, 99, **99**

H
Hackberry, 36, 105, **105**
Hamamelis, 56, 58-59, 113, **113**
Hardiness and climate, 16-17
Heart's Delight, 99
Hedera, 113, **113**
Hedges, as windbreaks, 41-43, **42**, **43**
Helianthemum, 114, **114**
Hemerocallis, 49, **48-49**, 60, **60**, 114, **114**
Hen-and-chickens, 123, **123**
Herbicides, 87
Herbs, 28, 30, 70-71, 93
Heuchera, 27, 50, 60, **50-51**, 114, **114**
Hibiscus, 59, 89
Honey Locust, 18, 36, 59, 113, **113**
Honeysuckle, Trumpet, 36, 117, **117**
Hornbeam
  American, 105
  European, 105, **105**
Hosta *(Hosta),* **4**, 27, 82, 84, 114, **114**
Hot conditions, 32-36
Houseleek, 123, **123**
Hyacinth
  Grape, 117, **117**
  Wood, 66, 67
Hydrangea *(Hydrangea),* 24, 26, 89

I
Iberis, 36, 52, **52-53**, 114, **114**, 115, **115**
Impatiens *(Impatiens),* 60, 64, **65**, 115, **115**

Indigo, Blue False, 17, 102, **102**
Integrated Pest Management (IPM), 92
Intensive planting, 81, **81**, 82
Invasive plants, 12
Iresine, 26, **26**, 64
Iris *(Iris),* 15, **15**, 37, 46, **46-47**, 115, **115**
  Siberian, 46, **46-47**, 115, **115**
Ivy
  Boston, 36, 119, **119**
  English, 48, 49, **48-49**, 113, **113**

J
Jacob's-ladder, 121, **121**
June Grass, 116, **116**
Juniper *(Juniperus)*
  Chinese, 115, **115**
  Creeping, 26, 115, **115**

K
Koeleria, 116, **116**

L
Lactuca, 73, 116, **116**
Lamb's-ears, 32, **32**, 124, **124**
Larkspur
  Annual, 107, **107**
  Rocket, 36, 92, 107, **107**
Lathyrus, 116, **116**
Laurel, Mountain, 6, 89
Lawns, 19-22, **22**, 34, 35, 68, 84, 97
Layering plants, 82
  (see also Overplanting)
Lepidium, 108, **108**
Lettuce, Garden, **28**, 29, 73, 116, **116**
  Leaf, **28**, 52, **52**, 73, **73**
Liatris, 116, **116**
Light, in garden design, 14
Lily *(Lilium),* 18, 66, 82, 116, **116**
  Asiatic Hybrid, 116, **116**
  Tiger, 116
Lily-of-the-valley, 27, **27**, 48, **48-49**, 107, **107**
Lobularia, 117, **117**
Lolium, 22, 96
Lonicera, 36, 117, **117**
Lungwort, 17, 121, **121**

M
Maiden Grass, 117
Maidenhair Tree, 113, **113**
Manure, 12, 48, 72, 77
Maple, 22, 26, 56
  Amur, 36, 99, **99**
  Hedge, 99, **99**
Marguerite
  Blue, 111
  Golden, 18, 46, **46-47**, 100, **100**
Marigold, 65, 94
  Cape, 109, **109**
  Marsh, 14, 38, 104, **104**
Meadow Rue, 125, **125**
Miscanthus, 117, **117**
Moisture, in garden design, 15
Moss, Rose, 36, 121, **121**
Mulch, 33, 34, 35, **35**, 61, 79, 84, 85, **85**, 86, 87, 92, 95
Muscari, 117, **117**
Myrica, 117, **117**

N
Narcissus *(Narcissus),* 66, 67, **67**, 82, 118, **118**
Nemophila, 118, **118**
Nettle Tree, 105, **105**

O
Obedient Plant, 17, 50, **50-51**, 120, **120**
Oenothera, 12, 118, **118**
Onion, 29, 52, **52**, 53, 71, 82, 93, 118, **118**
  Flowering, 67
Oregano *(Origanum),* 70, 71
Overplanting, 18
  (see also Layering plants)
Overseeding, 22
Oxydendrum, 50, 51, 118, **118**

P
Pachysandra *(Pachysandra),* 19, 67, 119, **119**
Paeonia, 16
Pampas Grass, 108, **108**
Panicum, 119, **119**
Papaver, 16
Parsley, 52, **52-53**, 70, 119, **119**
Parthenocissus, 36, 119, **119**
Paths, 30-31, **30**, **31**, 34, 38, 48

Pea
  Garden, 72, **72**, 73, 81, 82, 119, **119**
  Perennial, 116, **116**
  Snow, 119
Peat moss, 12, 40, 76
Pelargonium, 64
Pennisetum, 120, **120**
Peony, Garden, 16, 82
Peppergrass, 108, **108**
Pepper, 29, 73, 82
Perennials, 60-62
Periwinkle, 19, 22, 126, **126**
Permanent-mulch garden, 28, 29, **29**
Pest control, 28, 67, 92-95, **92-93**
Petroselinum, 119, **119**
Petunia, 41, 65
pH, 13, 76, 77, 78
Phalaris, 120, **120**
Phaseolus, 102, **102**
Phormium, 120, **120**
Physostegia, 17, 50, **50-51**, 120, **120**
Pink
  Deptford, 109
  Maiden, 97, 109, **109**
Pisum, 119, **119**
Plans, garden, 48-53
Plant groupings, in garden design, 18
Plant hardiness zone map, 127
Plantain Lily, 114, **114**
  Fragrant, 114
Planting, 20, **20**, 33, **33**, 80-83
Platycladus, 57
Platycodon, 120, **120**
Polemonium, 121, **121**
Polygonatum, 13, **13**, 121, **121**
Polygonum, 50, **50-51**, 121, **121**
Poppy
  California, 52, **52-53**, 110, **110**
  Iceland, 16
Portulaca *(Portulaca),* 14, 36, 41, 96, 121, **121**
Privet, 41, 42
Pruning, 89-91
Pulmonaria, 17, 121, **121**

Q

Quaking Grass, 103, **103**
Queen-of-the-meadow, 111
Queen-of-the-prairie, 111, **111**
Quercus, 56, 58, **58**, 59, 59

R

Radish, 29, 73, 122, **122**
Raised beds, 15, 28, 37, 40, **40**, 79
Raphanus, 122, **122**
Redbud, 106, **106**
Reed Grass, 21, **21**, 104, **104**
Regional calendar of garden care, 96-97
Repellent plants, for pest control, 28, 93
Resistant vs. tolerant plants, 92
Rhododendron, 6, 23, **24**, 58, **58**, 89
Rhubarb, 73, **80**
Rhus, 36, 122, **122**
Ribbon Grass, 120, **120**
Rockspray, 36, 108, **108**
Root-bound plants, 80
Rose
  Rock, **14**, 114, **114**
  Sun, 114, **114**
  White Rock, 17
Rose *(Rosa)*
  Rugosa, 36, 42, 50, **50-51**, 122, **122**
  Saltspray, 122, **122**
Rose-of-Sharon, 59, 89
Rosemary, 28, 94
Rudbeckia, 36, 122, **122**
Ryegrass, 22, 68, 96, 97

S

Sage, 28, 94
  Bethlehem, 121
  Jerusalem, 121, **121**
  Mealy-cup, 52, **52-53**, 123, **123**
  Scarlet, 17, 123
  Tricolor, 64
Salvia *(Salvia),* 17, 52, **52-53**, 63, **63**, 64, 65, 123, **123**
Sapphire Flower, 103, **103**
Scilla, 16, 123, **123**
Sea-holly, Alpine, 110, **110**
Seashore conditions, 41-43
Sedum, 123, **123**
Self-seeding plants, 61, **61**, 62, **62**, 70-71

Sempervivum, 123, **123**
Senecio, 123, **123**
Serviceberry, 42, 56, 58, 100, **100**
Shadbush, 100, **100**
Shallot, 52, **53**, 124, **124**
Shelter belts, 41-42
Shredded bark, as mulch, 79
Shrubs, 6, 18, 23-25, **23**, **24**, **25**, 26, 43, **43**, 56-59, 78, 89
Silene, 124, **124**
Silver Lace Vine, 50, **50-51**, 121, **121**
Silver Mound, 49, **48-49**, 101
Snakeroot, Black, 107, **107**
Soaker hoses, 34, 41, 84-85, **84-85**, 86
Soapweed, 36, 126, **126**
Soil, 12-13, **13**, 15, 25, **25**, 28, 76-79, 87
Solarization of soil, 87
Solomon's-seal, 13, **13**, 121
  Fragrant, 121, **121**
Sourwood, 50, **51**, 118, **118**
Speedwell, 125, **125**
Spiderwort, 125, **125**
Spindle Tree, Winged, 111, **111**
Spirea, Blue *(Caryopteris),* 46, 47, **46-47**, 105, **105**
Spirea, Bumald *(Spirea),* 57, 124, **124**
Sporobolus, 124, **124**
Spurge, 111, **111**
  Cushion, 36, 111
  Japanese, 119, **119**
Squill, Siberian, 16, 123, **123**
Stachys, 32, **32**, 124, **124**
Stonecrop, 123, **123**
Succession planting, 82
Sumac, 36
  Shining, 122
  Smooth, 122, **122**
  Winged, 122
Sundrops, 12, 118, **118**
Switch Grass, 119, **119**

T

Tassel Flower, 110, **110**
Thalictrum, 125, **125**
Thuja, 57
Thyme *(Thymus),* 30, 34, 50, 51, **50-51**, 52, 53, 70, 125, **125**
Tomato, 14, 29, 53, 72-73, 82

Torenia, 125, **125**
Tradescantia, 125, **125**
Transpiration, 32
Traps, for pest control, 92, 93-94
Trees, 56-59, 78, 82, 83, **83**
Trumpet Creeper, 12, 36, 104, **104**
Tulip, 66, 82, 93
Turkey-foot, 100, **100**
Turtlehead, 106
  Pink, 106, **106**

V

Valerian, Greek, 121, **121**
Vegetables, 28-29, **28**, 72-73
Verbena
  Desert Sand, 99, **99**
  Sand, 99
Veronica *(Veronica),* 46, **46-47**, 62, **62**, 125, **125**
Viburnum *(Viburnum),* 16, 24, **24**, 126, **126**
Vinca *(Vinca),* 19, 22, 126, **126**
Violet *(Viola),* 13, **13**
  Sweet, 126, **126**
Violet, Bush *(Browallia),* 103, **103**

W

Warm-climate plants, 17
Watering, 84-86
Weeding, 87-88
Wet conditions, 37-40
Widow's Tears, 125, **125**
Windbreaks, 23, 41-42, **42**, 43, **43**
Wishbone Flower, 125, **125**
Witch Hazel, 56, 58-59, 113, **113**
Woodruff, Sweet, 19, 70, 112, **112**
Wormwood, 101, **101**

Y

Yew, 6, 23, 56, **56**
Yucca, 36, 126, **126**

Z

Zebra Grass, 117, **117**
Zelkova, Japanese *(Zelkova),* 56, 126, **126**
Zone map (plant hardiness), 127